GW01110785

MAN vs LIFE
A Strategic Approach to Man Stress™

Very Basic Coping Skills for Very Basic Men

ROB PEGLEY

MURDOCH BOOKS

Contents

Introduction	8
The World Is Changing	9
Social Concerns	10
Anxiety Dashboard	11
Maybe It's Just Me....	12
Identification	16
SWOT Analysis	17
360° Feedback	18
Brand Pyramid	19
Shit Sandwich Syndrome	20
Unhealthy Escapes	21
Lotto Daydream	22
External Scan	23
Alignment	24
Oh, And You're Going To Die...	25
Background Analysis	26
When We Were Born	27
Vital Signs?	28
Chinese Years	29
What We Are Called	30
What We Wanted To Be	31
School Performance	32
Juvenile Concerns	33
The Getting Years	34
Conclusions	35
Man Strategy	38
Basic Man Strategy	39
Man Goals	40
SMART Objectives & KPIs	41
Short vs Long Term	42
The Dual Horizon	43
A Perfect Schedule	44
Conclusions	45
Health	48
Weight	49
Man Food	50
Pie Pie Chart	51
Veg Bell Curve	52
Diets	53
Alcohol	54
Dr Google	55
Sick Roadmap	56
Dentist No-Go	57
Fitness Activities	58
Gym Etiquette	59
Mental Health	60
Spirituality	61

Sex & Relationships	62	**Real Man's Stuff**	92
Love/Sex/Friendship Zones	63	Cars: An Idiot's Guide	93
Wife Mapping	64	DIY: Difficulty/Praise Ratio	94
Sex/Masturbation Frequency	65	DIY: How Handy Are You?	95
Sex/Masturbation Venues	66	Garden: Tool/Fun Ratio	96
Getting Sex	67	Fashion: What We Wear	97
Man vs Venus	68	Fashion: Textbook Errors	98
Marriage Problems	69	Grooming Basics	99
The Divorce Gap	70	**Man Time/Leisure**	**100**
Worlds Collide	71	Family Activities	101
Kids	**72**	Holiday Matrix	102
Pregnancy & Birth	73	Evenings Out	103
Stress Graphs	74	Hobbies Criteria	104
The Business Case	75	Pyramid of Desire	105
Baby Jobs	76	Are You Chef-Like?	106
The Books Don't Say…	77	Music	107
Org Charts	78	Comfort Films	108
School Roadmap	79	Books We Read	109
Exxy Curricular	80	How Techy Are We?	110
Party Mapping	81	Why We're Still Highbrow(ish)	111
Xmas Gift Inflation	82	**Conclusions & Next Steps**	**114**
Bedtime Stories	83	Summary	115
Career & Finance	**84**	We're Not This	116
Disposable Income	85	So What Are We Really?	117
Job History	86	Next Steps	118
Daily Intensity	87		
Taking a Sickie	88		
Work Toilets Stress	89		
Sea Changes?	90		
Mortgage Stress	91		

"Frankly, the stress is starting to get to you and there must be another way to live. How did your 20s turn into this?"

Introduction

9   The World Is Changing
10   Social Concerns
11   Anxiety Dashboard
12   Maybe It's Just Me…

The World Is Changing

NB: The world pictured is actually the current one, prior to expected change.
Source: Every PowerPoint ever created about social media or the GFC.

Social Concerns

Society faces a number of major issues...

- **Global Warming** — 58
- **World Poverty** — 54
- **The War on Terror** — 70
- **Middle Eastern Conflict** — 66
- **Increasingly Secular Society** — 59
- **Debt Crisis in Europe** — 86

⬅······· Level of Concern % ·······➡

Source: No real basis to the percentages, it's just a vibe based on how concerned the newsreaders look when discussing these things.

Anxiety Dashboard

But frankly there is enough to worry about closer to home...

	PROBLEMS LISTED IN ORDER OF RECURRING THOUGHTS	LIFE CATEGORY	POSITION LAST WEEK	HOW WORRIED?
1	Money. Will there ever be a time I don't worry about it?	Financial	1	
2	Death. (Although at least it would end money worries...)	Meaning of Life	3	
3	What comes after death? Freaks me out even briefly thinking about it.	Meaning of Life	2	
4	Is that a new mole or have I always had it?	Health	-	
5	Drinking too much. Try and keep to weekends only. And possibly Thursdays.	Health	8	
6	Unspecific feelings of impending doom. (Linked to number 5?)	Health	7	
7	Presentation needs to be finished by Friday, haven't even started yet. Will wing it.	Career	-	
8	Blackout at work drinks. Did I really say that to boss, or dream it? (See 5, again.)	Career / Health	-	
9	Need to see dentist. Can feel weird cavity when flossing. Must drink less Diet Coke.	Health	18	
10	Got to lose weight. Definitely starting new diet. On Monday.	Health	5	
11	Bit constipated again. Must replace morning muffins with All Bran. From Monday...	Health	17	
12	Think the wife is a bit fed up with me again. Must try harder to talk and stuff.	Relationships	14	
13	Need to clear out garage. Wife has been on about it for months. Looks fine to me.	Relationships	19	
14	Car making strange rattling noise again. No wonder mechanic has just gone to Bali.	Car / Financial	-	
15	What do the people who work for me think of me? Keep seeing them whispering...	Career	16	
16	Will they discover I've accessed porn on my work laptop? (Blame kids?)	Career	9	
17	Has the youngest got Asperger's? Or is he just ignoring me all the time?	Kids	11	
18	Does oldest child have ADHD? Or is she just mucking about in class too much?	Kids	13	
19	Can't get rid of ants. Now they're in the bathroom too. Tiny, smelly little bastards.	DIY	20	
20	Foxtel Planner down to '23% Free'. Clear all kids' iCarly stuff before World Cup.	Leisure	-	

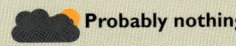

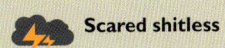

Probably nothing   Fairly worried   Scared shitless

With all that going on in my head it's amazing I can sleep at night. (Insomnia was actually at number 12, but dropped out this week after upping red wine intake.)

Maybe It's Just Me....

So is it just me, or do you all feel a bit lost too? **At 23 I was bulletproof**. I was different. My life would be different, my relationships (if I ever got round to having a lasting one) would be different. My job, my musical tastes, my dress sense – they would all be different. Most of all, **I'd be different to my parents**. With their cosy little house and their boring lives, watching TV and pottering in the garden. I would never be like that. Now, I should be so lucky. **Overrun by kids and work and financial stress, all I crave sometimes is a 'boring life' with some peace and quiet.** The simplicity of life my grandparents seemed to have.

Gen X. **We were the generation that had it all**. Given a massive head start by our baby boomer parents, who worked their arses off in the shadow of two world wars, so that we could blow it. **We wanted it all**: education, travel, portable careers, consumer goods, active sex lives; then when we'd exhausted our limited imaginations, we finally wanted the wife, mortgage, kids and conformity that our parents arrowed in on from Day One. And we wanted it now. **Instant gratification** in pursuit of any of our newly desired goals. And if we had to **stick it all on a credit card**, we'd do it. And if the credit card turned into a loan, then so be it. **Our parents started with nothing, they grafted and were patient and they slowly built a secure life**. We pissed it up against the wall before having a crack ourselves. Now my parents stay up late sharing meals with friends; their mortgage paid off and my Dad retired at 56. There's no way I can afford to stop work before I'm 65, by which time I'll probably be stacking shelves in Coles; forced out of the corporate environment in my late fifties as **I become an embarrassment to the Gen Y bosses** I now probably work for. My only mates that have done well for themselves adopted the tactics of my parents: ignored uni, went straight to work and bought a house while I was still drinking cheap beer in the Student Union. Now they own their own businesses and invest wisely.

Too intellectually superior to believe in God, too apathetic to protest against anything, **we weren't sure what we believed in**, other than having a good time. Besides, science has all the answers, doesn't it? (Even if we don't know what they are ourselves.) And anyone who believes in alien life forms is a nut (more intellectual superiority), despite the fact we live in an infinite and ever-expanding universe that we will never live long enough to explore. **Death is the only real inevitability** in our lives and yet we behave as though it'll never happen. We all accept that if we aren't furthering mankind's legacy by the time we're in our late 20s then we'll need to find other, shallower pursuits to justify our existence; and so we try to see better films than each other, discover better bands than each other and drink in cooler places than each other. We all become mini critics, slating films we have no idea how to make and criticising bands when we can't play an instrument (intellectual superiority again). And yet we know somehow that deep in our core **we're better than all of these people**, we just haven't proved it yet.

Then kids come along. The income gets bigger, but so do the outgoings. In fact, the **outgoings now seem to outstrip the income**, but it just about seems manageable. The strain of those early years as a parent affects all areas of your life. **You hardly ever go out** as a couple and when you do, you end up talking about the kids. When you go out with mates you try to cram a month's worth of hedonism into one night and it takes you a week to recover. **You complain about having less and less sex**, and then you complain about it less and less. The kids grow up. They want more and more, and although they have far more than you ever had, it never seems enough. You move up the ladder at work, and each time you move up the **job gets a bit harder, you earn a bit more cash, but you spend a bit more cash**. Eventually you decide you've gone far enough, and perhaps you'd actually like an easier ride, but suddenly you're trapped by finance and family expectation and **there's no escape**.

You watch *Grand Designs* and *Escape to the Country* and dream of living in the middle of nowhere, but you'd need a stack of cash to pull it off and so **you'll need to stay in the rat race** for at least another decade. **You'd like to build your own place but you can just about put together IKEA cupboards.** Your dad could change the gearbox in his car, while you sometimes pay someone to clean it. Your shallow pursuits are still there, but they all seem to revolve around food now: finding better restaurants, drinking better wine, drinking cooler beers, or finding a slightly better hummus. **If you can't escape to the country, then just escape in a bottle of red.** And one bottle becomes two. At least it takes away your anxieties, until they hit you full in the face the next morning. You dream of winning the Lotto; on really bad days you dream of living in a bedsit. **You're getting older.** You may never be as fit as you once were, you may never look as good as you once did, and you will certainly never fit into size 32 jeans ever again. You want to lose weight and you've tried every diet known to man, but sometimes it seems that food and drink are the only avenues of pleasure left open to you and you feel cheated without a curry and a glass of cab sav. **You're desperately holding onto a job you don't even want** and dreams of the Lotto have given way to dreams of a redundancy package. You think you'd quite like the sort of sex that you see sometimes on porn websites, although it looks far more aggressive than you remember, with all its frantic rubbing and spitting and what have you. And the girls you see at work seem more intimidating than when you were in your 20s, with their fake tans and enhanced bra technology.

And the noise. The never-ending sound of kids screaming and arguing and whining and not putting their clothes on and not taking their clothes off and not doing their homework and **answering back and dropping crumbs** everywhere. **So you stomp around the house cursing and doing the Loud Tidy Up.** And yet they're growing up so fast that you can already see a time when they might not need you anymore. We're decent blokes, though, and we try to **do the right thing.** We work hard, we know right from wrong, we try to be good husbands and fathers and we know what that involves. We're not the vacuous man-children that the adverts portray. We know how to cook, we know how to wash up, we know how to use the washing machine and we know what a sanitary towel is. **But we're not SNAGs**. And although we love footy, women and beer we're not Blokey or Laddish either. **We're not vain enough to be metrosexuals, but we dress well enough and have the odd bit of product**. We're not dogmatic enough to be Grumpy Old Men either, but we're starting to see where they're coming from. **We're Gen X that have lost our way slightly.** Gen Execs suffering from Man Fatigue, but somehow keeping it all together.

Frankly, the stress is starting to get to you though and there must be another way to live. **How did your 20s turn into this?** And yet you've got the kids, you've got the two cars, you've got the house, you've got the gym membership, the life insurance, the giant TV, the iPhone, Foxtel, wi-fi, the big silver fridge, the four-burner BBQ. **But something is not quite right.** Something is missing and **you can't quite put your finger on what it is**. But you know intuitively that you didn't think you'd ever feel like this when you were 23.

But as I say, maybe it's just me...

Let's say you did identify with even some of this diatribe, then maybe you'll gain something from this book. **There's a chance we have something in common** and can benefit from some shared truths. **If that's the case, then let's begin by analysing the current situation.**

Note to self: Wrote this when a bit drunk, might want to tone it down slightly...

MAN VS LIFE

Identification

17 SWOT Analysis
18 360° Feedback
19 Brand Pyramid
20 Shit Sandwich Syndrome
21 Unhealthy Escapes
22 Lotto Daydream
23 External Scan
24 Alignment
25 Oh, And You're Going To Die...

SWOT Analysis

STRENGTHS

- Got all of my teeth
- Got most of my hair
- Well-paid job
- Reasonable health
- Good standard of living
- Parents alive
- Healthy kids
- Take family holidays
- Still married
- Live in Australia, best country in the world
- Two cars
- Still got some Super
- Got a big TV and Foxtel
- Short drive to work

WEAKNESSES

- Overweight
- Drink too much
- Bit anxious (and even paranoid lately)
- Money worries
- Small house
- Time poor
- Dodgy left knee (old footy injury)
- Need reading glasses
- Allergic to fish
- Think I may be gluten intolerant
- Drink too much coffee
- Not sure my new boss likes me
- Mild asthma

OPPORTUNITIES

- Could get a new job
- Could go to the gym more regularly
- Could detox
- Could start drinking decaf
- Could get some therapy
- Could buy Lotto ticket
- Could budget for things better
- Could follow better diet
- Could start yoga
- Could sell possessions and become Buddhist monk
- Could fake own death

THREATS

- Drinking gets out of control, resulting in loss of family, career and dignity
- Wife decides she's had enough (who could blame her?)
- Nervous breakdown
- Lose job (and no redundancy)
- Kids tell people how grumpy you really are
- Obesity-related illnesses over time
- New boss doesn't actually like you

On the surface all looks well, but the weaknesses are real and the threats pretty genuine. The opportunities are all easily pursuable, but drinking decaf seems about as likely as the Buddhist monk thing...

360° Feedback

In a multi-source assessment from interested stakeholders there seemed to be a contradictory nature to some of the feedback...

KIDS
'Dad needs to take a chill pill. He's always chucking a spaz about manners or being tidy. Even leaning on the fridge door drives him nuts. Just calm the farm, Dad. Epic fail!'

BOSS
'He's motivated and pro-active. He displays a high-performance, team-based work ethic.'

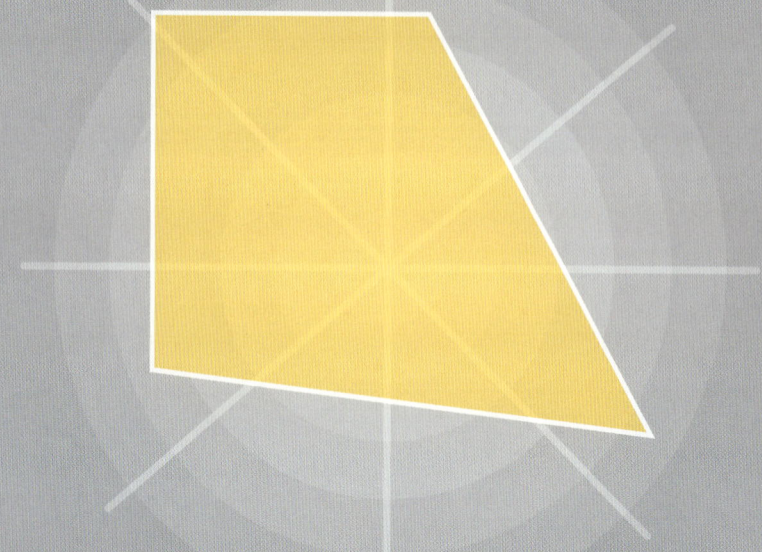

MATES
'Good bloke. Always gets the first beers. Pretty laid back, likes the footy, he's a top mate.'

WIFE
'He's a decent man, he works hard and he's a good Dad. He just doesn't seem all that happy these days. He just seems to find fault with everything.'

Brand Pyramid

The essence of the meaning to your life can be defined by building a brand pyramid.

FACILITATE FAMILY LIFE*

*(Albeit slightly grudgingly at times)

Likes a beer
Likes to watch sport
Will do anything for the kids
Enjoys the security of home
Works to live   Wants an easy life

Works hard to make a career
Drives people around   Fires up the BBQ
Provides family with finance
Puts bins out and changes light bulbs
Helps with homework   Looks after TV remote control

BRAND ESSENCE
In 2–3 words, what you really stand for

BRAND VALUES
Your core values & beliefs

BRAND ATTRIBUTES
The benefits you provide

Clearly you have attributes that prove useful to the consumer (your wife and kids), but alignment is not total. This can lead to self-pity arising when bandwidth is low, manifesting as statements such as 'You're only nice to me when you want something' or 'I'm not a bloody taxi'.

Shit Sandwich Syndrome

This lack of efficacy created by the misalignment of your values and ultimate function can lead to a displacement of feelings.

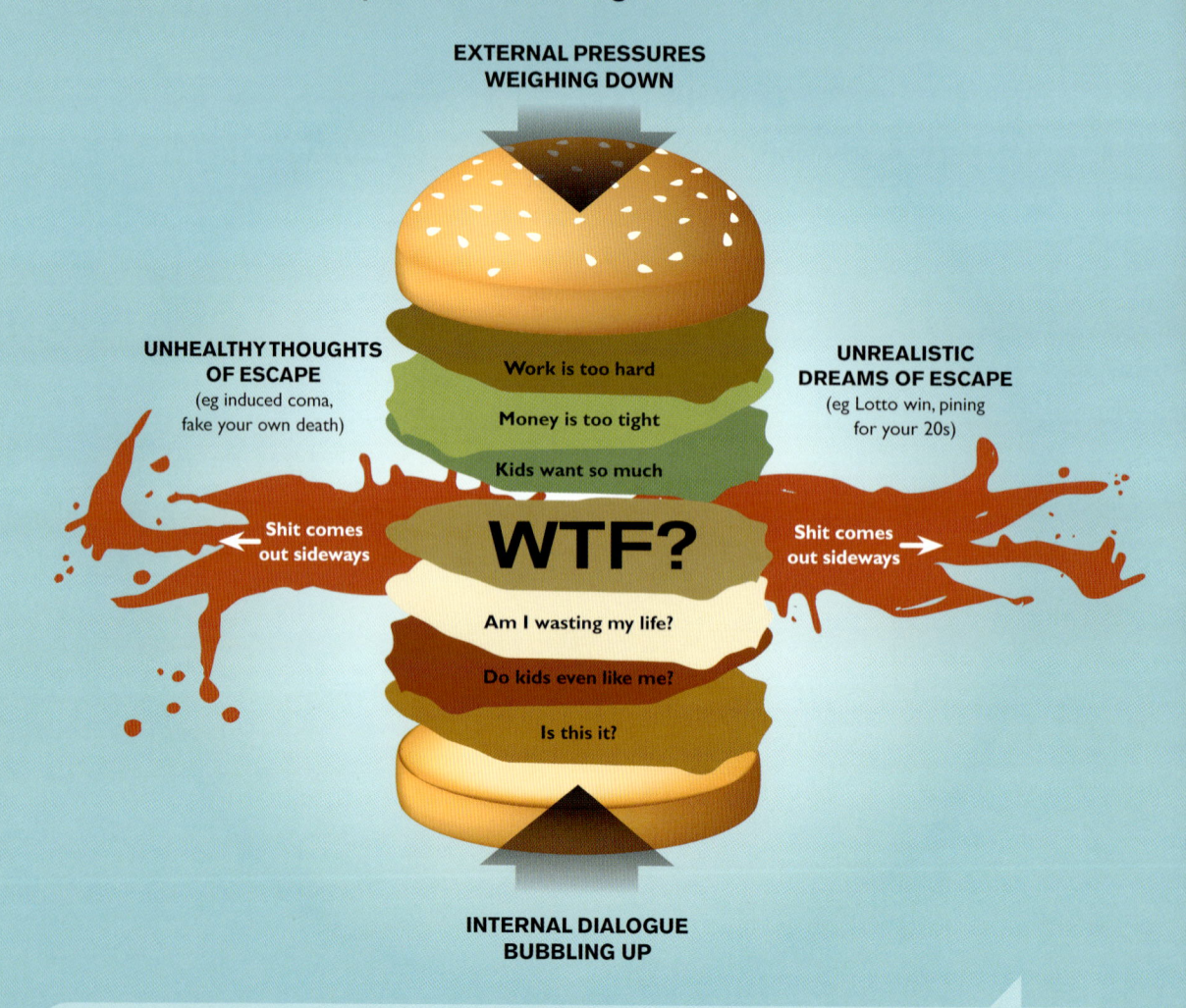

EXTERNAL PRESSURES WEIGHING DOWN

UNHEALTHY THOUGHTS OF ESCAPE
(eg induced coma, fake your own death)

UNREALISTIC DREAMS OF ESCAPE
(eg Lotto win, pining for your 20s)

Work is too hard
Money is too tight
Kids want so much

Shit comes out sideways ←   **WTF?**   → Shit comes out sideways

Am I wasting my life?
Do kids even like me?
Is this it?

INTERNAL DIALOGUE BUBBLING UP

Crushed between the convergence of internal dialogue and external pressure, the crap comes out sideways.

Unhealthy Escapes

In moments of extreme frustration (possibly fuelled by an excess of alcohol, or a lack of intimacy) thoughts of escape can become almost sinister in their negativity.

Short-term Coma

Admit it, every time you read about someone coming out of a coma, or being put in a medically induced coma, a tiny part of you feels jealous. Three months of peace and quiet, being fed by a drip. Wake up to your favourite music being played by sympathetic friends around the bed; 20 kg lighter, fully detoxed and with more sleep than you've had since you were a teenager. What's not to like about a short coma?

Bedsit

If you ever get divorced you'll be in a bedsit anyway. The wife and kids will get the house, the money, the dog and the big TV. You'll get the debts, the sofa bed and a studio flat, which is small enough to put your bread in the toaster without getting out of bed in the morning. Grim though it sounds, you sometimes sneak a glance on property websites at rental prices. Possibly after a kid's birthday party held at home.

Fake Your Own Death

That canoe bloke got away with it for years; he just got sloppy and complacent. Leave your shoes and clothes at the top of a cliff, then bugger off to Bali. Obviously there are certain drawbacks, such as leaving the kids to a life of trauma, anxiety and poverty. On the plus side, you don't have to finish that report for Accounts by Monday.

Bear Grylls Lite

How hard can it be? Fashion a shelter in the woods near the holiday park you visited last summer. Set up a little camp fire, give up shaving and live off fish and small animals you catch with your bare hands. Mosquito-bitten and scared, you'd be watching Foxtel in a holiday park cabin within 48 hours.

Just Give Up and See What Happens...

When it all seems too much, just refuse to get out of bed. Stop going to work, stop paying the bills, go bankrupt, let the wife and kids leave and just see what happens. It wouldn't be that bad, would it? Yes, it would. Pull yourself together, man.

Lotto Daydream

We've all thought about winning the Lotto at great length and have even considered the logistics to some degree. Whether to completely furnish the new place (including TVs, kids' toys and new clothes) before moving in, or move in with your crappy IKEA stuff and refurnish slowly over time. These thoughts occupy our minds in the morning traffic jams. The debates around how much it would take to give up work, and how much you'd give family and friends, depends on a) your starting point pre-Lotto win, and b) how tight you are.

AMOUNT	GIVE UP WORK	FIRST PURCHASE	TREAT YOUR PARENTS	APPROACH TO WINNINGS
100,000	👎	Bottle of champers	Small holiday	Pay off the credit cards, take a decent holiday, treat your family and then stick the rest in the bank.
500,000	👎	Crate of champers	Big holiday	Pay off the mortgage, take a decent holiday, treat your family and then stick the rest in the bank.
1,000,000	👎	Week's holiday	World cruise	Pay off the mortgage, buy a flash car, treat your family and then stick the rest in the bank.
2,000,000	👍	Month's holiday	Motor home	Pay off the mortgage but become fairly miserly in a bid never to have to work again.
10,000,000	👍	Indefinite holiday	Holiday home	Pay off mortgage, buy a flash car, stick wads in the bank and live off the interest. Golf and fine wine forever…

Odds of winning the top prize in Tuesday's Oz Lotto are about 45 million to one, so there is more chance of being hit by lightning. The reassuring thing to remember is that people do often get hit by lightning. So, every cloud and all that…

External Scan

They say that the grass is always greener on the other side of the fence... because there's more shit for it to grow in. By examining the micro-environment (your mates) we can see whether there is any truth to this.

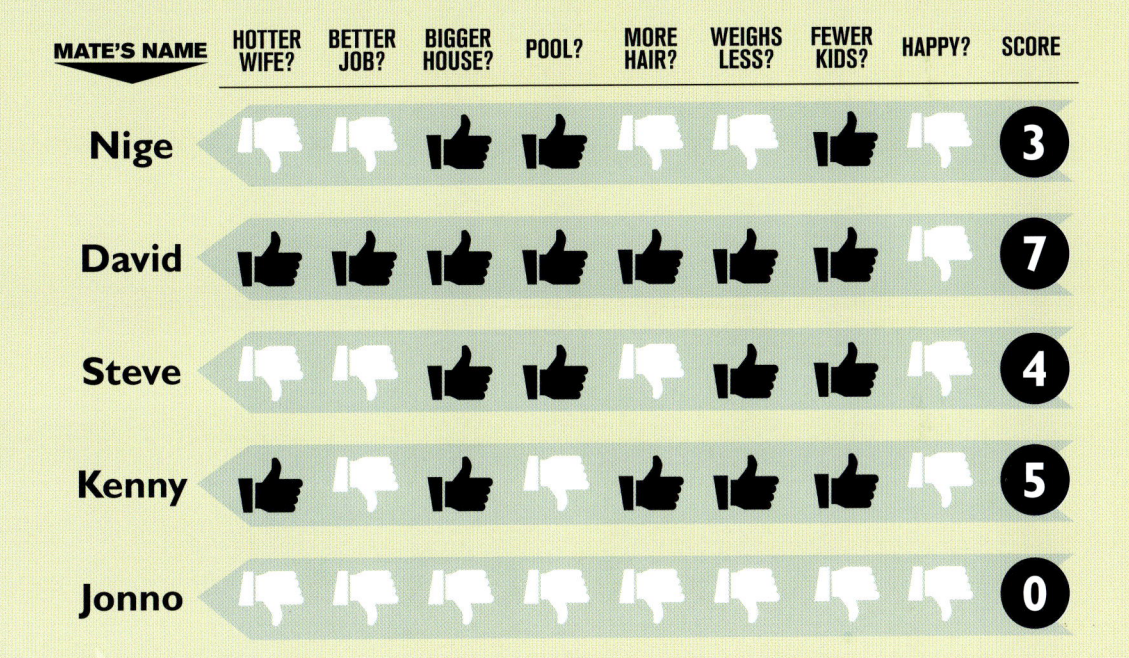

MATE'S NAME	HOTTER WIFE?	BETTER JOB?	BIGGER HOUSE?	POOL?	MORE HAIR?	WEIGHS LESS?	FEWER KIDS?	HAPPY?	SCORE
Nige	👎	👎	👍	👍	👎	👎	👍	👎	3
David	👍	👍	👍	👍	👍	👍	👍	👎	7
Steve	👎	👎	👍	👍	👎	👍	👍	👎	4
Kenny	👍	👎	👍	👎	👍	👍	👍	👎	5
Jonno	👎	👎	👎	👎	👎	👎	👎	👎	0

Average scores tend to be fairly similar among the core group of mates and there are some interesting findings: notably that David is a smug bastard who you should stop hanging around with. Even with his so-called perfect life, however, he still doesn't appear to be happy.*

The other major takeouts are a) that nobody seems to be particularly happy, and b) Thank God for Jonno being around or we'd all lose the will to live...

*NB: Sour grapes on our part may be throwing David's results. He does actually seems pretty happy on the face of it.

Alignment

The closer you identify with the hot spots on this mapping tool, the more likely you are to identify with this book.

| AGE | 20 | 25 | 30 | 35 | 40 | 45 | 50 | 55 | 60 | 60+ |

| KIDS | 1 | | 2 | | 3 | | 4 | | 5+ |

| SIZE | Slim | Average | Chunky | Obese | Massive |

| MIND | Relaxed | Anxious | Stressed | Manic | Cuckoo |

| FIT | Athlete | Fit | Lethargic | Slob | Clinically Dead? |

| FEEL | Blissful | Content | Restless | Irritable | Angry |

So for once it may actually suit your needs to be a stressed and irritable chunky fortysomething with a couple of kids...

Oh, And You're Going To Die...

Yes, we act like it's never going to happen. We bind ourselves to soulless social constructs to avoid contemplating the inevitable. Many of us even read on the bus simply to stop thinking about death. But it's going to happen, so we'd better crack on with things.

Best Countries for Life Expectancy (Males)*

1. Iceland *80.2*
2. Israel *80*
3. Switzerland *80*
4. Hong Kong *79.4*
5. Singapore *79*
6. Japan *79*
7. Australia *78.9*
8. Sweden *78.7*
9. Macau *78.5*
10. Canada *78.3*

*Source: United Nations (Yes, a proper source, not a stupid little extra joke.)

Most Common Causes of Death in Males (Australia 2009)*

1. Heart disease
2. Tracheal and lung cancer
3. Strokes
4. Chronic respiratory disease
5. Prostate cancer
6. Dementia, Alzheimer's and... now, where was I?
7. Colon/Rectal cancer
8. Blood and lymph cancer
9. Diabetes
10. Suicide

*Source: Australian Bureau of Statistics (Another proper source. This is bordering on proper research. Rest assured it won't happen again in the book.)

A heart attack at 79 would be okay, wouldn't it? It almost sounds comforting. Chronic respiratory disease is the one that sounds scary.

Background Analysis

27 When We Were Born
28 Vital Signs?
29 Chinese Years
30 What We Are Called
31 What We Wanted To Be
32 School Performance
33 Juvenile Concerns
34 The Getting Years
35 Conclusions

When We Were Born

Around 77 billion people are estimated to have lived before the first kid to be born in the Gen X era popped out around 1965. By the time Men at Work released *Down Under* Gen Y were on the way.

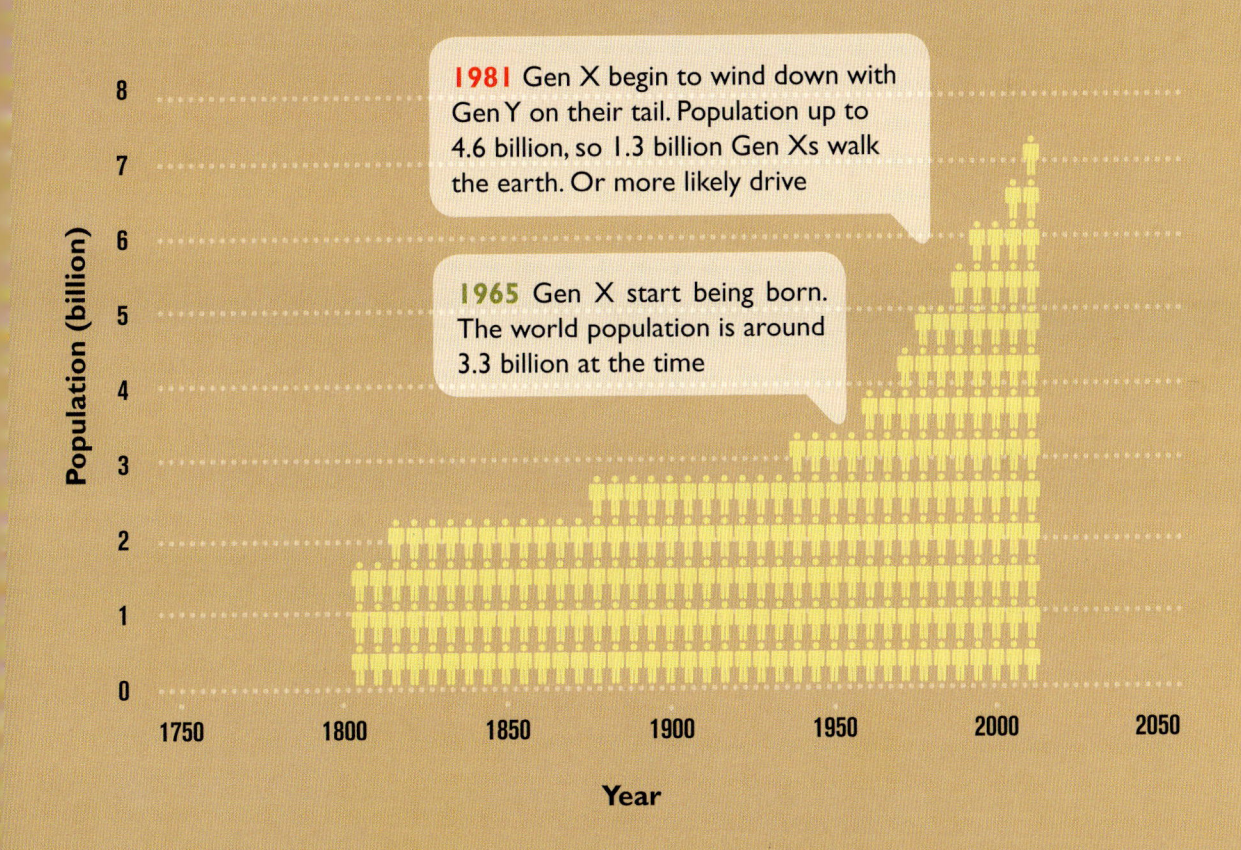

1981 Gen X begin to wind down with Gen Y on their tail. Population up to 4.6 billion, so 1.3 billion Gen Xs walk the earth. Or more likely drive

1965 Gen X start being born. The world population is around 3.3 billion at the time

Hard to decide whether it's ultimately comforting or alarming to be so relatively meaningless. On the one hand it's incredibly hard to be special; but there's also less historical pressure when it all starts going pear-shaped.

Vital Signs?

We don't believe in them, do we? You're due to be a Leo, then your mum has a Caesarian a day early and suddenly you're a Cancer. You're kidding us, right?

Aries	Taurus	Gemini	Cancer
Childish	Sulky	Nosy	Moody
Leo	**Virgo**	**Libra**	**Scorpio**
Jammy	Fussy	Loud mouth	Power crazy
Sagittarius	**Capricorn**	**Aquarius**	**Pisces**
Tactless	Workaholics	Bleeding hearts	Two-faced

Yes, we'll look at the odd horoscope (and ignore it, if we don't like it), but as for star sign compatibility, they're having a laugh. Self-perpetuating stereotypes drummed into us by older female relatives. (The author is an Aries, by the way.)

NB: The star sign descriptions are random and were made up by the author on a whim.

Chinese Years

We have even less confidence in this stuff. Everyone born in 1968 is a monkey. Of course they are. Having said that, we give it the time of day because the Chinese seem quietly and mysteriously more intelligent than us.

Dog
狗

Feb 6 1970 – Jan 26 1971

Dragon
龍

Feb 13 1964 – Feb 1 1965
Jan 31 1976 – Feb 17 1977

Horse
馬

Jan 21 1966 – Feb 8 1967
Feb 7 1978 – Jan 27 1979

Monkey
猴

Jan 30 1968 – Feb 16 1969
Feb 16 1980 – Feb 4 1981

Ox
牛

Feb 3 1973 – Jan 22 1974

Pig
猪

Jan 27 1971 – Feb 14 1972

Rabbit
兔

Feb 11 1975 – Jan 30 1976

Goat/Sheep
羊

Feb 9 1967 – Jan 29 1968
Jan 28 1979 – Feb 15 1980

Rat
鼠

Feb 15 1972 – Feb 2 1973

Rooster
鷄

Feb 17 1969 – Feb 5 1970
Feb 5 1981 – Jan 24 1982

Snake
蛇

Feb 2 1965 – Jan 20 1966
Feb 18 1977 – Feb 6 1978

Tiger
虎

Jan 23 1974 – Feb 10 1975

> Monkey and Dragon sound best; Pig and Rat have a stigma. All the rest are much of a muchness. Let's move on.

What We Are Called

Not too many of our Gen X same-age friends are called Jayden, Mason, Kyle, Jared, Tyler, Logan, Caleb or Xavier.

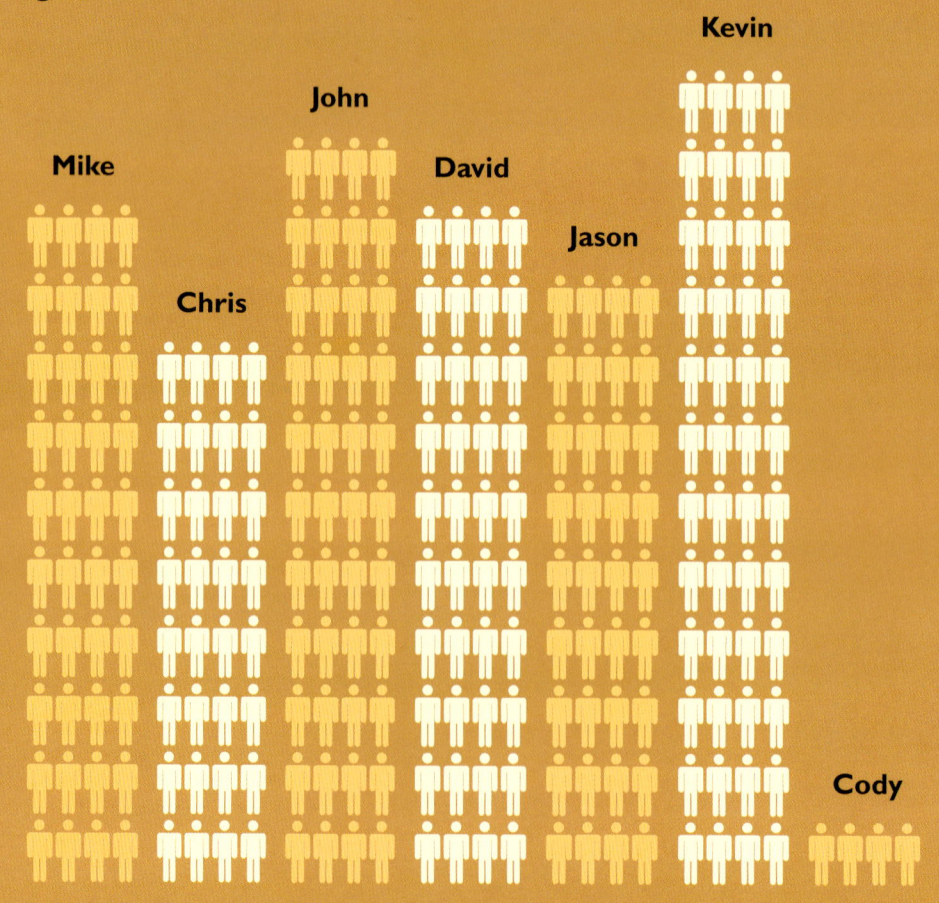

Mike · Chris · John · David · Jason · Kevin · Cody

And interestingly, the more secular society has become, the more religious the names we've chosen for our kids: Jacob, Joshua, Ethan, Noah, Joseph, Samuel... Birthday party invitations are like a book of psalms.

What We Wanted To Be

MAN vs LIFE

In early life our predicted career choices were bold, physical and involved travel and conflict. Everything we avoid in our careers now.

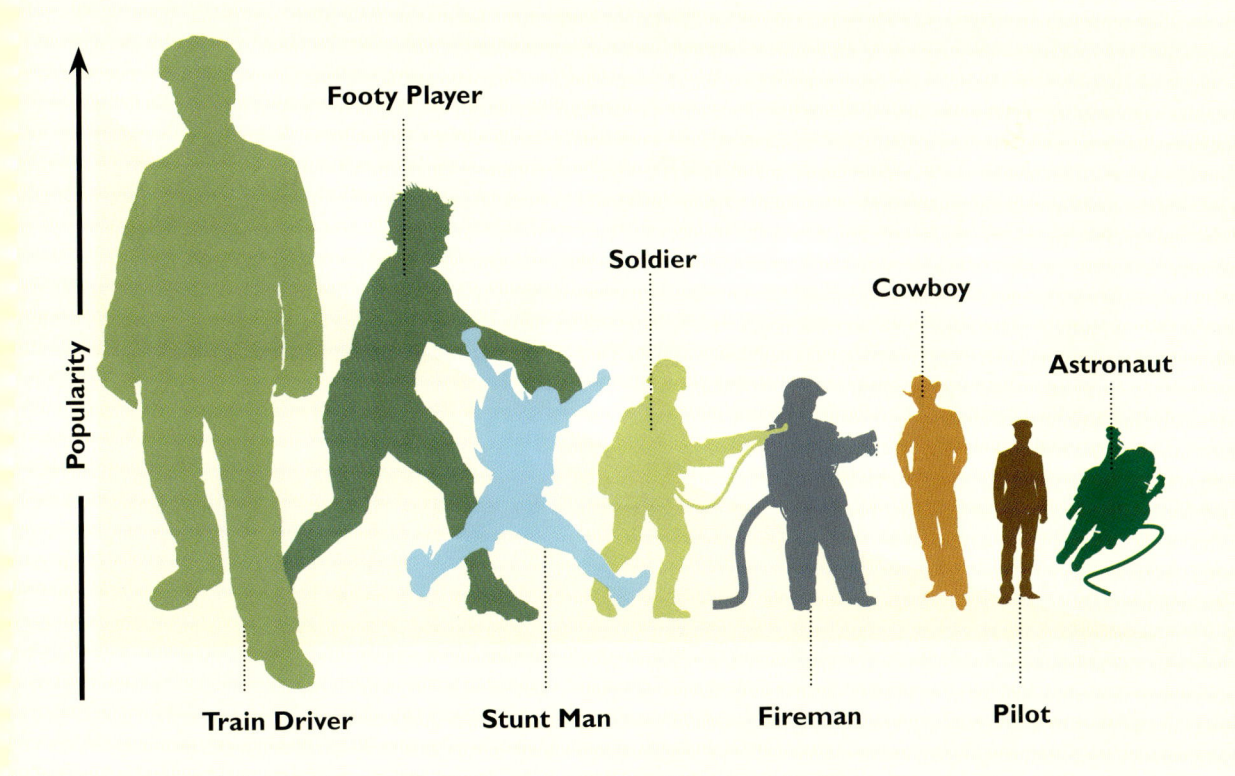

↑ Popularity

- Train Driver
- Footy Player
- Stunt Man
- Soldier
- Fireman
- Cowboy
- Pilot
- Astronaut

Interestingly, External Auditor, Funds Manager, Systems Analyst and Data Warehouse Consultant did not figure highly in our childhood plans.

School Performance

When evaluating educational achievement there seems to be a severe decline in effectiveness around the age of 15. This is known in academic circles as: discovering girls and booze.

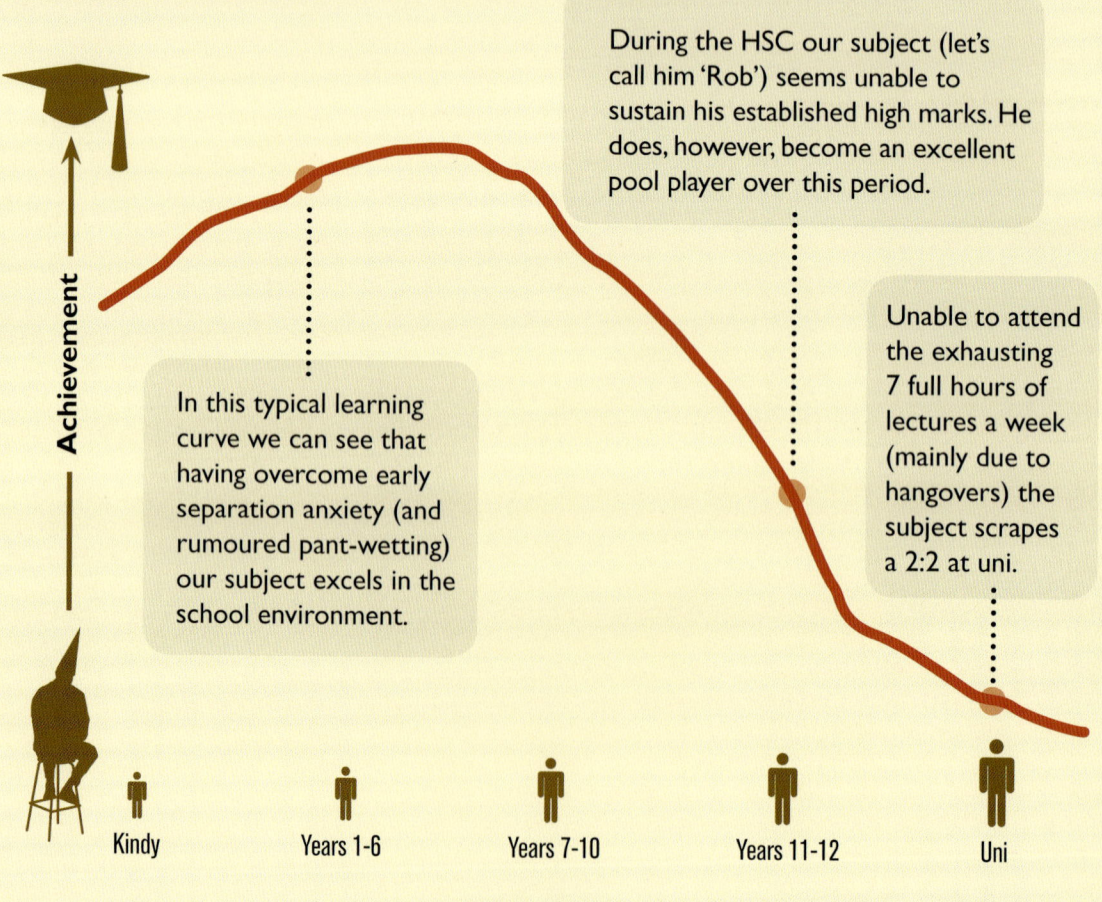

During the HSC our subject (let's call him 'Rob') seems unable to sustain his established high marks. He does, however, become an excellent pool player over this period.

In this typical learning curve we can see that having overcome early separation anxiety (and rumoured pant-wetting) our subject excels in the school environment.

Unable to attend the exhausting 7 full hours of lectures a week (mainly due to hangovers) the subject scrapes a 2:2 at uni.

Achievement

Kindy | Years 1-6 | Years 7-10 | Years 11-12 | Uni

School Years

A pattern for working life is being established during this process: forget the work/life balance, this is the hedonism/work balance...

Juvenile Concerns

Unlike the regimented Anxiety Dashboard of adulthood, childhood worries come randomly and continuously. And utterly heartbreaking though they might seem at the time, they're often forgotten the next day.

Wonder when this tooth will fall out? **Hope they don't laugh at my new haircut** *Lost fluffy panda, is it in the car?* **Do I have to have a bath?** Not that babysitter, she makes us go to bed at 7.30 **Only 50c from the tooth fairy! It's not fair** *Dad is always on at me to tidy my bedroom* **Hope I don't have to sit next to Marcia in class again, she smells of wee a bit** Must do my homework, got in trouble last time **Need money for more footy cards, falling behind mates** *PE tomorrow, hate changing, wish I had more pubes (but not as many as Pete)* **Can't believe I trod in dog shit in my new trainers, can't get it out of the tread** Need to hide my blazer in bag, no idea why mum makes me wear it when everyone else has a bomber jacket **Big spot on chin, will talcum powder cover it?** *Wish I could stay up later* **Why can't I have Coke?** Dean's mum lets him have chips way more than me **Wish Dad wouldn't tell me off in public** *Wish Mum wouldn't hug me in public* **Wish they both wouldn't sing in public** Not green beans for tea, do I really have to eat them? **Lid came off the pencil sharpener and everything in my pencil case is grey and dirty now** *Libby always gets more cake than me* **Hope I get the ZX Spectrum for Christmas** How come Will gets more pocket money than me? **But ALL of my friends have got one...**

> Generally, childhood anxieties are a weird mix of needing to conform with peers and being wildly oppositional to any parental advice.

The Getting Years

The late teens and early 20s are all about accumulating things and experiencing things for the first time. Even mundane things such as shaving (which later drives you insane) seem appealing.

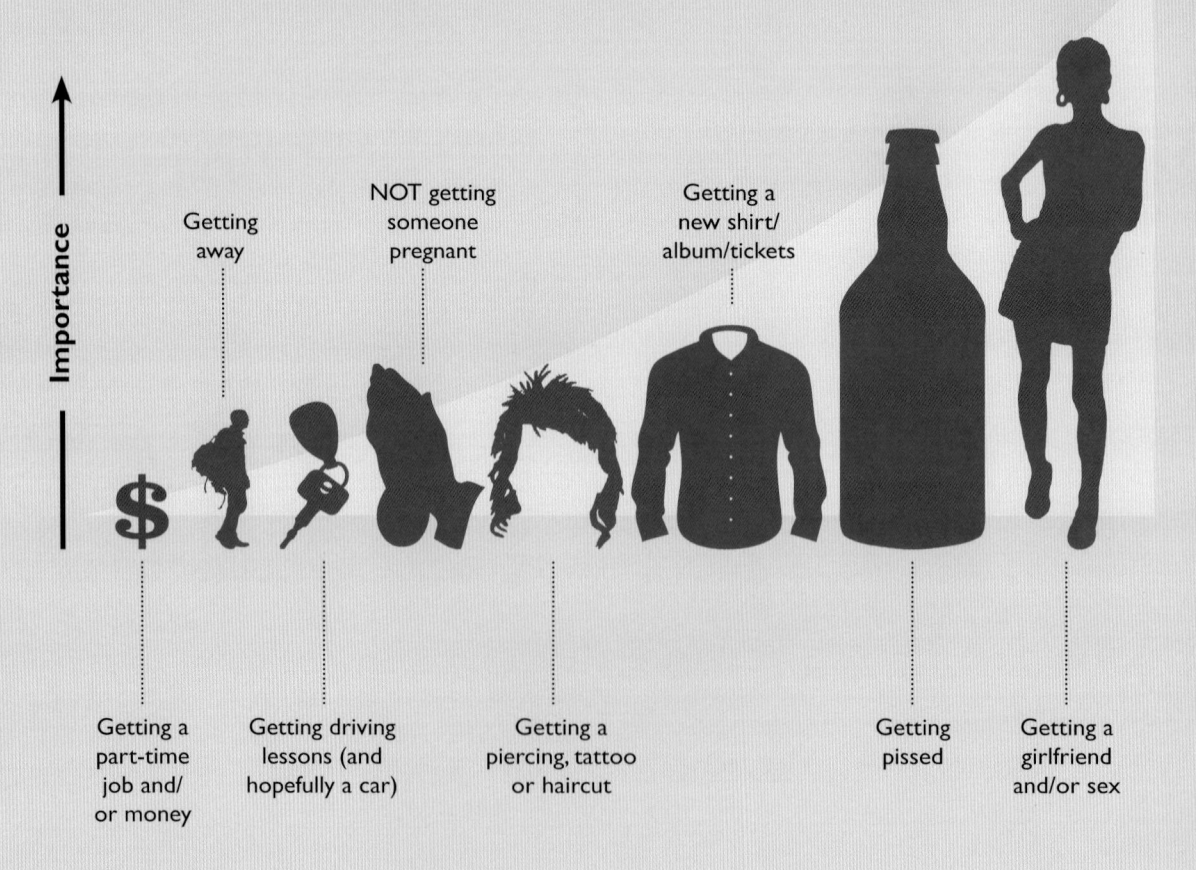

Importance ↑

- Getting a part-time job and/or money
- Getting away
- Getting driving lessons (and hopefully a car)
- NOT getting someone pregnant
- Getting a piercing, tattoo or haircut
- Getting a new shirt/album/tickets
- Getting pissed
- Getting a girlfriend and/or sex

> The irony is that later in life some of this runs in reverse. After years of trying to avoid getting someone pregnant, there comes a point where you try to work out if you're actually capable of doing it.

Conclusions*

'Well, at one point you've got it, and then you lose it and it's gone for ever'. Sick Boy's Unifying Theory of Life from the film *Trainspotting* is as true for any of us as it is for the downward trajectory of Lou Reed's and Sean Connery's careers. Only in childhood do we have the very basics of life that we later lose and never get back: a complete lack of fear, fully abandoned fun without consequences, wasting time without guilt and any concept of responsibility. It's sheer abandon and naivety, free from the bondage of self. A bondage that will gather pace as you gain awareness of how the world really works. If you could go back to that child or teen and give them some advice, it would be pretty simple:

- Be careful when you're pissed. Don't climb on big stuff, don't cross busy roads carelessly, or jump into water when you don't know how shallow it is; don't have unprotected sex. It seems fun at the time, but that stuff can really ruin your life.
- The stuff you're worried about now, you'll hardly even remember when you're in your 30s.
- Qualifications aren't as important as you think they are.
- Your parents are on your side.
- Have a crack at learning an instrument while you have spare time.
- Keep playing sport and don't give it up for anything. Anything.
- Buy property as soon as you can. Rent it out if you don't want to be tied down. And don't get tied down too soon, either.

Hardly an exercise in thought leadership, but these simple life lessons provide a framework for the reckless. They are hardest to remember after a few beers, which paradoxically is when you need them most.

*NB: This page is free from humour as the author was overcome by melancholy and remorse.

"It will help if you visualise your goals: picture yourself at 78 kg in new $300 ASICS, running under the Harbour Bridge with the fresh glow of having had sex, while thinking about a beer with mates later. It's such a good image, why spoil things by actually attempting it?"

Man Strategy

39 Basic Man Strategy™
40 Man Goals™
41 SMART Objectives & KPIs
42 Short vs Long term
43 The Dual Horizon
44 A Perfect Schedule
45 Conclusions

Basic Man Strategy™

The vision underpinning Man Strategy™ can be broken down into four broad goals encompassing Quality Time, Slush Fund, Sex and An Easier Life. Existing strategies to achieve these goals are often vague.

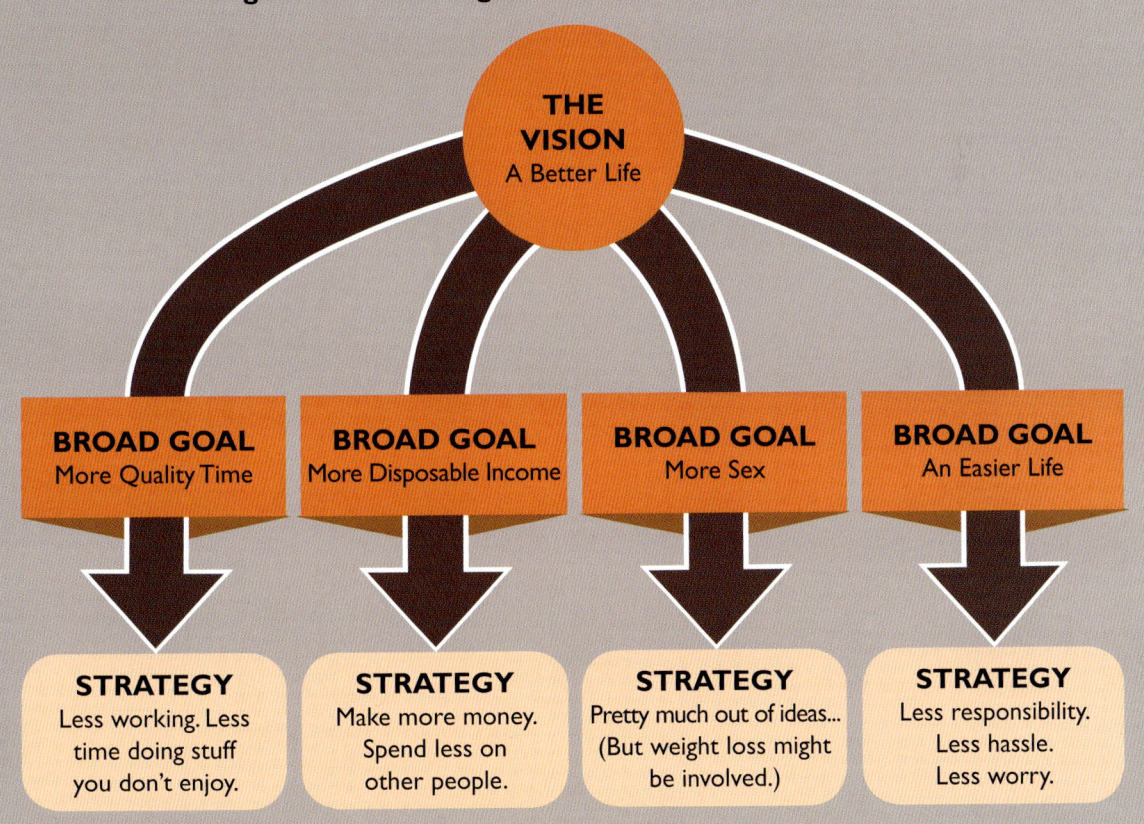

THE VISION
A Better Life

BROAD GOAL
More Quality Time

BROAD GOAL
More Disposable Income

BROAD GOAL
More Sex

BROAD GOAL
An Easier Life

STRATEGY
Less working. Less time doing stuff you don't enjoy.

STRATEGY
Make more money. Spend less on other people.

STRATEGY
Pretty much out of ideas... (But weight loss might be involved.)

STRATEGY
Less responsibility. Less hassle. Less worry.

Vision and strategy are normally set in late December and implemented on the first Monday in January (New Year's Day is too harsh). Typically the plan runs until mid to late February. It is then abandoned for 10 months of wistful Blue Sky Planning ahead of next year's strategic push.

Man Goals™

Unlike Objectives, which are specific, Goals tend to be broad, general and intangible. Because they are abstract, they are hard to measure. We therefore prefer Goals to Objectives.

More Quality Time

If you're not at work then you're either cooking tea, clearing up after the kids, driving someone to a concert or sporting event or – worse still – sticking around to watch a concert or sporting event. This year it's all going to change and there's going to be more time for YOU. Time to watch sport, go to the gym, play golf and relax. But can you give Josh a lift to Eagle Tag first? (It's your turn to be referee as well...)

More Disposable Income

It would be nice to get an iPad2. And those new irons Chris has look far better than your old clubs. Be great to have a proper mountain bike too, not the $99 one you've got that ends with you literally pushing shit up hill. But first the kids need new uniforms; there's the school library fee (it says *optional* donation' on the form...); then car rego, music lessons, athletics fees... Might leave you enough for a bottle of red.

Lose Weight / Get Fit

If only you were the same weight you were when you were 22, then EVERYTHING would be better. Eat like a jockey and train like an iron man and it might be possible.

Have An Easier Life

Free from responsibility, free from hassle and free from worry. Just up your alcohol intake and all of this is possible. Unfortunately it negates the other four goals...

Have More Sex

So what if 'Mike and Sandra apparently hardly ever have sex', you're not Mike!

These (very) basic Goals look reasonable when taken at face value, but considering they have been the same unachieved goals for the last 10 years, we are right to be sceptical about their potential.

SMART Objectives & KPIs*

Specific, Measurable, Attainable, Relevant and Timely. If we're serious about self-improvement – and frankly, that's debatable – then we need more than just vague goals. We need specific objectives that are usually well beyond our capabilities, and which were probably set when drunk.

Quantifying More Quality Time

In six months time I will be playing golf once a week, going to the gym three times a week, taking a music lesson one evening per week, having Friday night out with the boys and having a weekend away every other month. If the wife leaves you after the first five months of this, then this may well be easier to maintain.

Quantifying Getting Fitter

I will run a half-marathon by the end of the year. At the very least I will look some up online and possibly enrol for one.

Quantifying More Disposable Income

I will spend $500 on myself every month. This will go on either clothes, sporting goods or techy gadgets. I will tell the wife it was $200, not $500, and I will keep the cash in a sock hidden in my golf bag.

Quantifying Weight Loss

I will lose 20 kg in 40 weeks – half a kilo per week. It sounds actually possible when written down like that, doesn't it...

Quantifying More Sex

We will have sex at least twice a week. Preferably on nights there's no sport on.

It will help if you visualise these goals: picture yourself at 78 kg, in new $300 ASICS, running under the Harbour Bridge with the fresh glow of having had sex, while thinking about a beer with mates later. It's such a good image, why spoil things by actually attempting it?

*NB: Don't actually set KPIs for this stuff – there's enough of that at work without beating yourself up further.

Short vs Long Term

With all of the strategies there will be a balance to be made of what takes you nearer to or further away from your goals and how much enjoyment you derive from the activity while engaged.

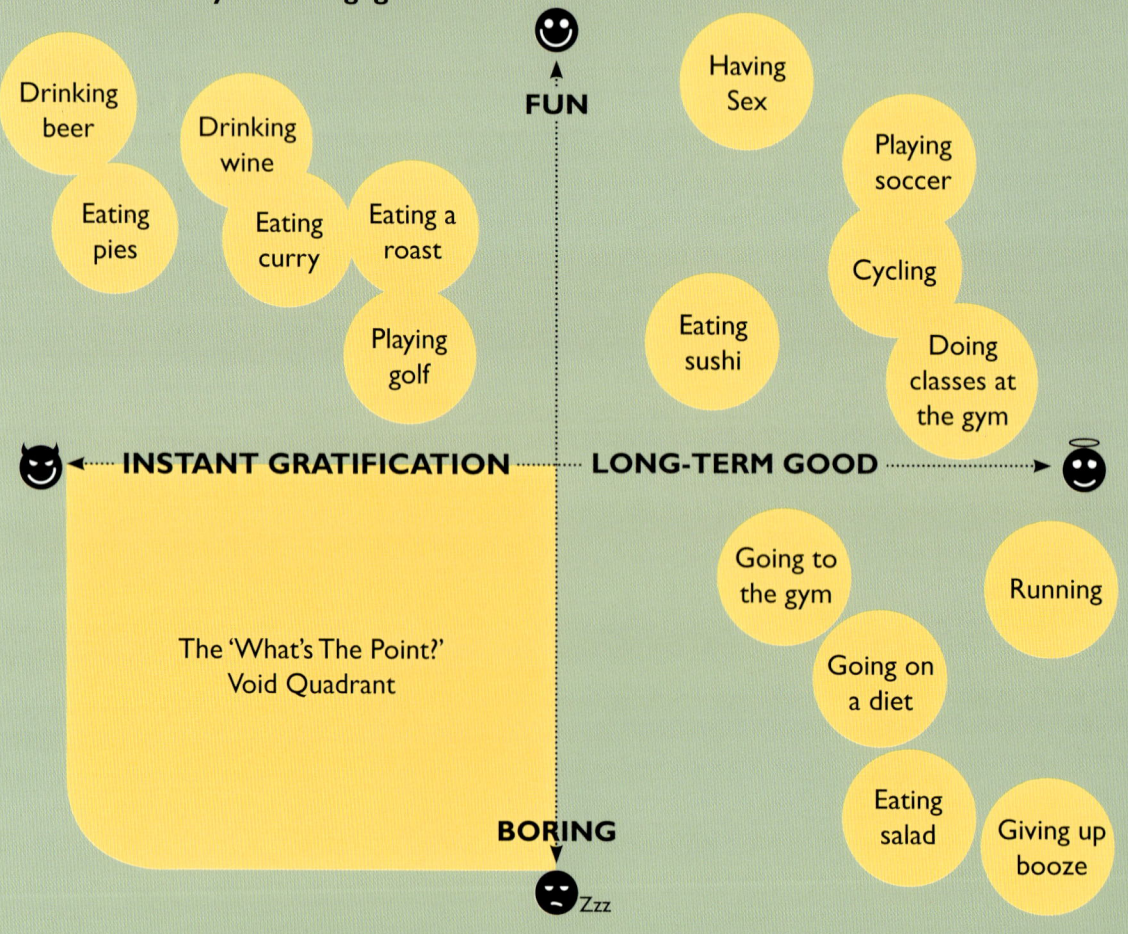

FUN

- Drinking beer
- Drinking wine
- Eating pies
- Eating curry
- Eating a roast
- Playing golf
- Having Sex
- Playing soccer
- Cycling
- Eating sushi
- Doing classes at the gym

◄──── **INSTANT GRATIFICATION** ········ **LONG-TERM GOOD** ────►

The 'What's The Point?' Void Quadrant

- Going to the gym
- Running
- Going on a diet
- Eating salad
- Giving up booze

BORING Zzz

> If you were a soccer player who had sex a fair amount of the time and drank little, then your weight problems would go away (eg David Beckham). If you just play golf and drink beer it will not (eg John Daly).

The Dual Horizon

There are long-term and short-term views to consider in how we live life: long-term is all about how and when we retire.

> Try to get a financial advisor on the case somewhere in your 30s. It's tax deductible. Even keep receipts if you go for a beer together. He'll know how to claim.

RETIREMENT

LIFE · WORK · KIDS

> The earlier you start thinking about your pension the better you'll be set up. Start thinking in your 20s and you'll be minted. But you've got to be some sort of tedious freak to even consider your pension at that age.

A Perfect Schedule

Transformation to The Perfect You is possible, but goes way beyond low-hanging fruit...

TIME OF DAY	Monday	Tuesday	Wednesday	Thursday	Friday	Saturday	Sunday
🌅	5 am: Vinyasa Flow at the beach	5 am: Thai boxing – spar with Snake	5 am: Ocean swim with the surf club	5 am: Triathlon training (work on transitions)	5 am: Karate (black belt refresher)	5 am: Tai chi followed by hatha yoga	5 am: 15 km run on the sand dunes
	Oatmeal flaxseed and blueberries	Scrambled tofu and mint tea	Soy protein shake and seeds	Spinach and papaya smoothie	Quinoa and rice milk porridge*	Millet and soy with goji berries	Poached egg as a treat
	Seal deal with the sustainable energy people	Present latest strategy to conference	Speech to the industry about new trends	Take core team on paintball bonding	Lunch for kids mentored this year	Golf with the boss (don't let him win)	Let wife lie in after making her breakfast
	Homemade brown rice sushi	Herbal soup with kiwi fruit	Mung bean salad	Chickpea and beetroot soup	Seven-bean salad with wheatgerm	Throw some corn cobs on the BBQ	Make organic roast for the family
☀️	Meditation straight from work	Last Japanese lesson of the term	Practise guitar for upcoming concert	Acupuncture session in Chinatown	Finish last chapter of book for agent	Try to do some painting to relax	Take the kids for a kickabout
	Millet pilaf with roasted peppers*	Lentil casserole	Rice pasta with nettle pesto	Courgette curry with brown rice	Take away! Chicken noodle soup	Asparagus risotto	Salad and small glass of red. Sunday!
	Help teach eldest son drums	Volunteer session at the soup kitchen	Bake cookies for kids fete tomorrow	Remember donation for kids' home	Clear big pile of ironing to help out	Invite mother-in-law for dinner	17th 6-month anniversary (bet she forgets)
	Help daughter with algebra revision	Leave spa voucher on wife's pillow	Take kids for late-night nature walk	Watch *Eat, Pray, Love* together	Buy wife new shoes online	*Sex in the City* marathon on TV	Get kids' uniforms ready for morning
🌙	Kama Sutra #3 The Turning Man	Kama Sutra #7 The Lower Union	Kama Sutra #5 The Touching Embrace	Kama Sutra #9 The Morning Star	Tantric sex for around three hours	Perform oral sex until wife exhausted	Night off to read our books together

This would appear to be unsustainable on a long-term basis. In fact, even a full day looks beyond our capabilities. Some men can barely remember their wife's name, let alone a 6-month anniversary.

*NB: Can someone also please explain what millet and quinoa are?

Conclusions

THE PERFECT YOU?

IT.
IS.
NEVER.
GOING.
TO.
HAPPEN.

> "It's amazing that men and women stay together for a month or two, let alone years on end, when you consider the lack of strategic fit…"

Health

49 Weight
50 Man Food
51 Pie Pie Chart
52 Veg Bell Curve
53 Diets
54 Alcohol
55 Dr Google
56 Sick Roadmap
57 Dentist No-Go
58 Fitness Activities
59 Gym Etiquette
60 Mental Health
61 Spirituality

Weight

After that 125 kg rock bottom (if ever there was a misnomer...) in your early 30s, when the kids were both really small, things are back on track. But the trend over time is up and the forecast is not good.

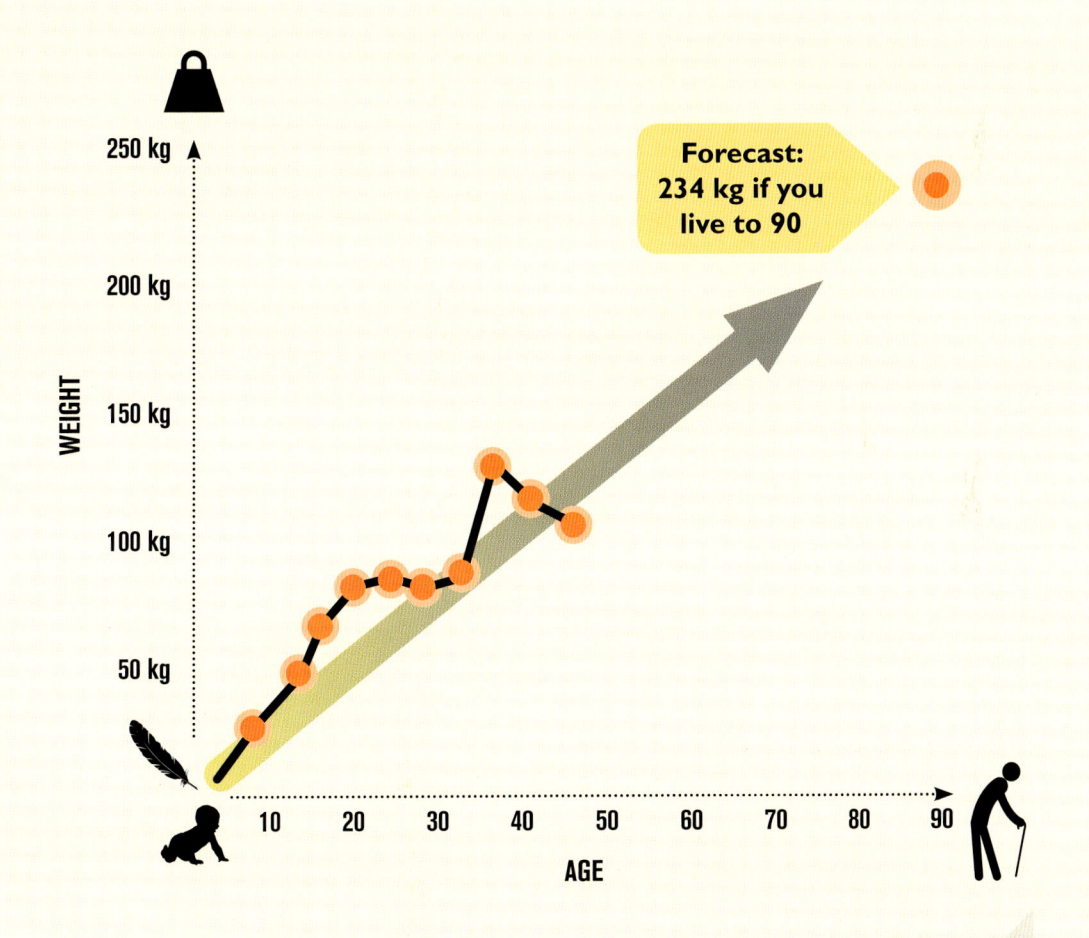

Forecast: 234 kg if you live to 90

Don't use the 'muscle weighs twice as much as fat' argument as that makes things worse. And **NEVER** work out your **BMI** – the utter horror has you reaching for the biscuits before you can say 'morbidly obese'.

Man Food

Is it any wonder that weight is an issue for us, when – given the chance – we would treat every meal time like it was our last day on death row? Most men share some common food traits.

WE LOVE MEAT — And we're not talking a thin slice of chicken breast. Steak, bacon, pork belly, crispy duck, sausages, burgers, ribs, hot dogs, kebabs. Thousands of years of evolution haven't stopped us from ripping the skin off a roast chicken as we carve it and looking up with a greasy, demented expression on our face when caught in the act.

WE LOVE COMFORT FOOD — Pies, pizzas, sausage and mash, roasts, Chinese take-away, shepherd's pie, anything in gravy, cooked breakfast, chips. You never see females queueing at the food court carvery, and there's no comfort in a rice cracker.

WE LOVE SPICE — Curries and chillis that give you a good sweat; hot-and-spicy pizzas; chilli-flavoured peanuts or dips. And we keep chilli oil and chilli flakes on hand for emergencies.

WE LOVE TOXINS — Beer, red wine, coffee, whisky, port. We're always winding ourselves up or down. We like food that gets our heart racing.

WE LOVE WEIRD TASTES — The phrase 'Yeah, I'll try that' is clearly a man thing. Pickled eggs, pork scratchings, curry pie. We'll even take things out of the bin in extreme circumstances.

WE DON'T LIKE... — Rice crackers with cottage cheese; or the idea that soup is a meal. We like salad if potato and bacon are involved and a runny egg is cracked over the top of it.

It need only be one night out of 365, but the text from the wife saying 'thought I'd do fish and salad for tea' lets you down quicker than that cheap blow-up mattress you took camping last year.

Pie Pie Chart*

If ever there was a strategy page resulting from a perfect storm, it would be the pie chart about men's favourite foods.

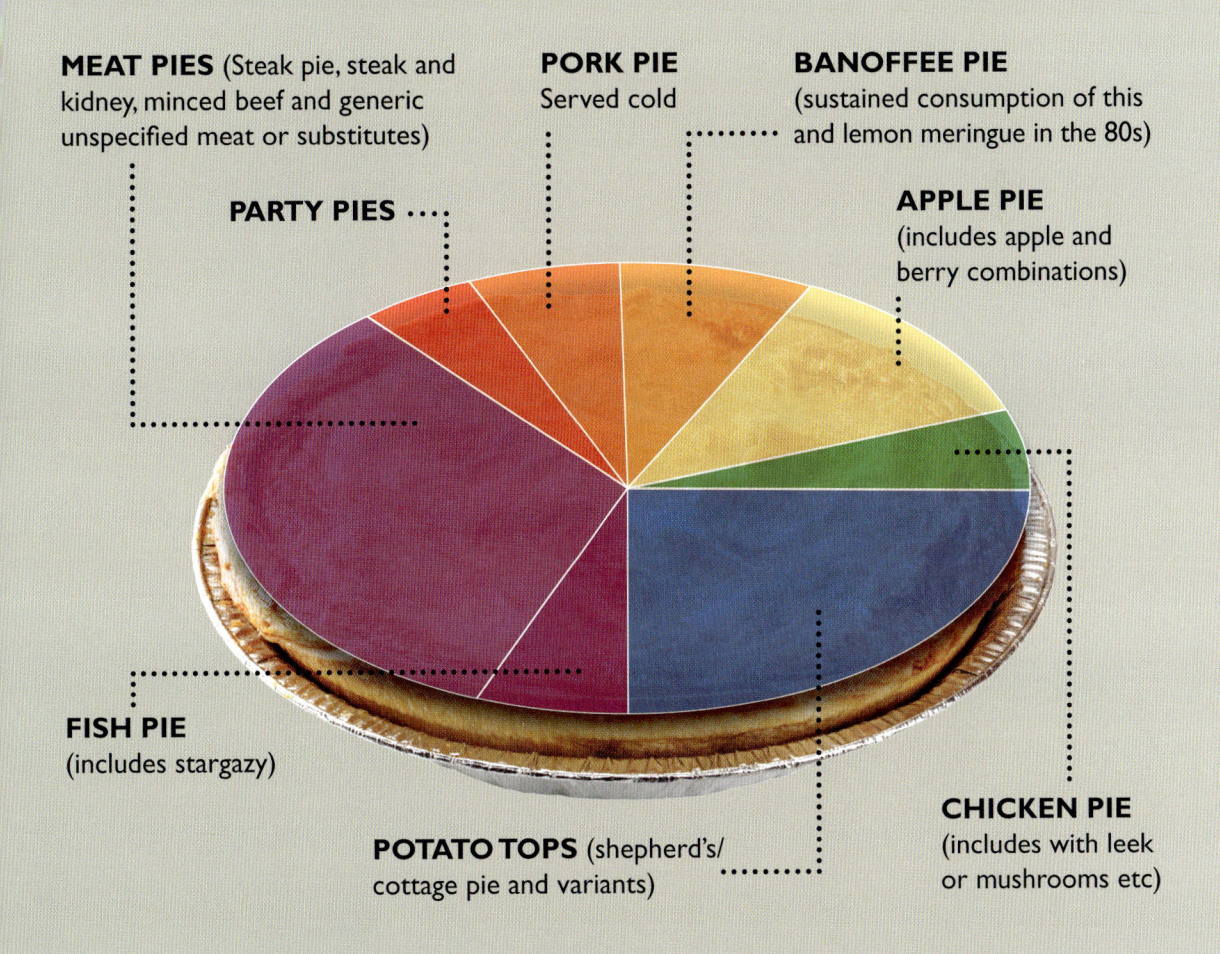

MEAT PIES (Steak pie, steak and kidney, minced beef and generic unspecified meat or substitutes)

PARTY PIES

PORK PIE Served cold

BANOFFEE PIE (sustained consumption of this and lemon meringue in the 80s)

APPLE PIE (includes apple and berry combinations)

FISH PIE (includes stargazy)

POTATO TOPS (shepherd's/ cottage pie and variants)

CHICKEN PIE (includes with leek or mushrooms etc)

Despite the definition of a pie as a baked dish of pastry encasing a filling, we have excluded pasties, samosas and – obviously – quiche from this important piece of research. Perhaps controversially we have allowed 'potato tops'.

*NB: The author would like to acknowledge that a pie pie chart is incredibly obvious but he could not pass up the opportunity.

Veg Bell Curve

An interesting phenomenon was observed in the course of this research: the discovery of the vegetable consumption bell curve.

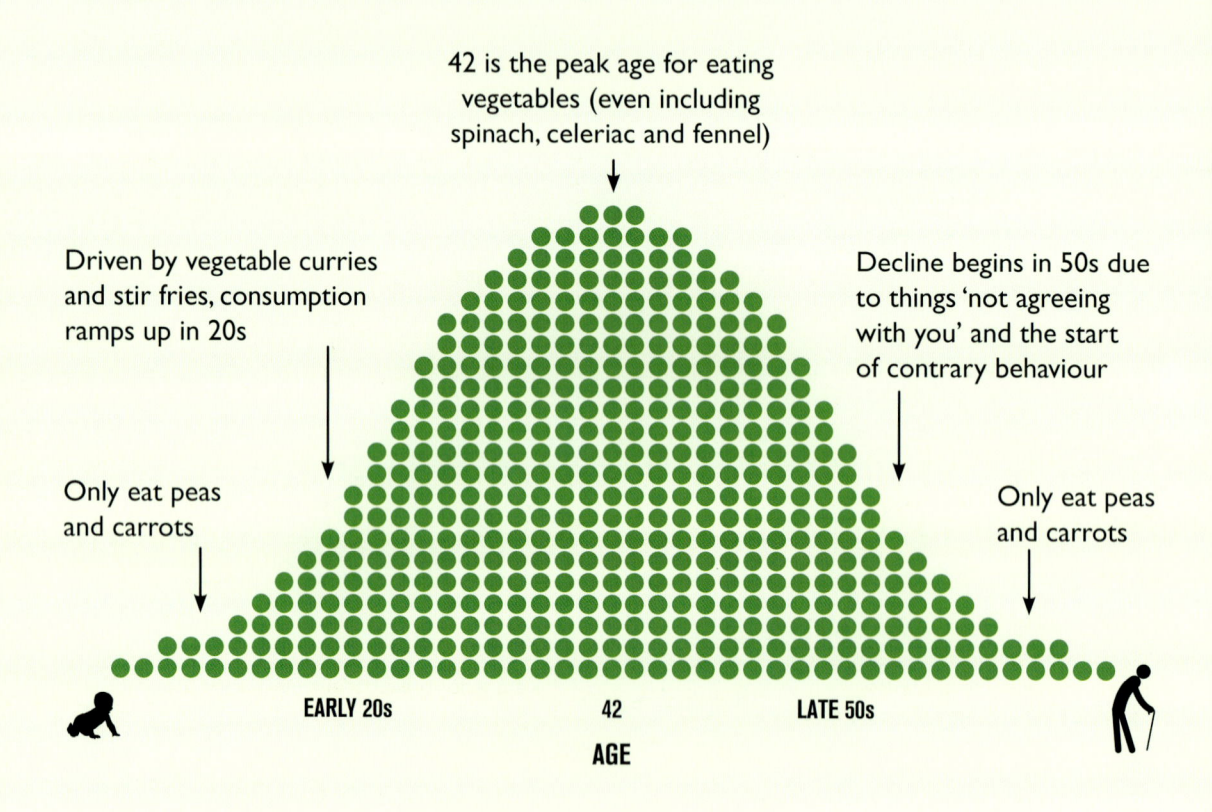

42 is the peak age for eating vegetables (even including spinach, celeriac and fennel)

Driven by vegetable curries and stir fries, consumption ramps up in 20s

Decline begins in 50s due to things 'not agreeing with you' and the start of contrary behaviour

Only eat peas and carrots

Only eat peas and carrots

EARLY 20s 42 LATE 50s

AGE

Men will do almost anything to disguise vegetables as 'real food'. This includes adding spice (cumin, coriander) to, say, carrots, or adding bacon and nuts to green beans and sprouts. In some cases vegetables are served in batter (tempura) or curried as a side dish. And, of course, the world is a better place as a result.

Diets

If you think about food a lot, then diets are an opportunity to focus on it pretty much 24/7. Here are a few diets you may have tried; they are all effective, although only if you actually stick to them.

DIET	GOOD BITS	BAD BITS	CHANCES OF STICKING TO IT*
Atkins	Steak, eggs, bacon, cheese, cream... duh!	No carbs. Not even fruit to start with.	Can only have been invented by a man. Quick weight loss initially, but surely you'll have a heart attack eventually?
Weight Watchers	Eat anything you want. There must be a catch...	Weighing food shows you how little you can eat.	One of the most sensible diets, which means slow weight loss. Requires patience. Like a jail sentence.
F-Plan	You won't get bowel cancer if you keep it up.	The food is boring and you fart constantly.	You'll sleep well, exhausted by the constant chewing. You may also die of fibre-induced boredom.
Blood Type	O-group diet is pretty good, a bit like Atkins.	It all seems a bit too complicated and scientific.	What if the wife and kids have different blood groups? It'll be a logistical nightmare for you all to follow.
Cabbage Soup	It only lasts a week.	Er, you eat cabbage soup for a whole week.	It's boring, it'll give you a headache and it is more about temporary water loss than shifting fat. But it's only a week...
Slim Fast	Simple, fast & convenient. Milk shakes are good.	Milkshakes are good, but twice a day...	A shake for breakfast and lunch and a 'normal meal' in the evening; we assume that isn't pizza and chips.
Don't Eat Crap	Eat whatever you want, apart from tasty stuff.	No pies, pizza, beer, chips, take-away, etc.	The diet most blokes attempt: 'I'm not really on a diet, I'm just trying to avoid eating crap'. Unlike the past 30 years...

Clear out the fridge and cupboards, do a healthy food shop, maybe get a detox kit, then one last Chinese takeaway. Make sure to binge when you've 'been good' and you can always start again on Monday...

*At over 100 kg, the author admits bitterly that your chances of sticking to these diets may be far better than he has stated.

Alcohol

Remember, fellow Weight Watchers: two bottles of red wine is only 15 points, so if you've had two coffees and a tin of chickpeas, you'll be within your limit for today. Could alcohol perhaps be a problem for you?

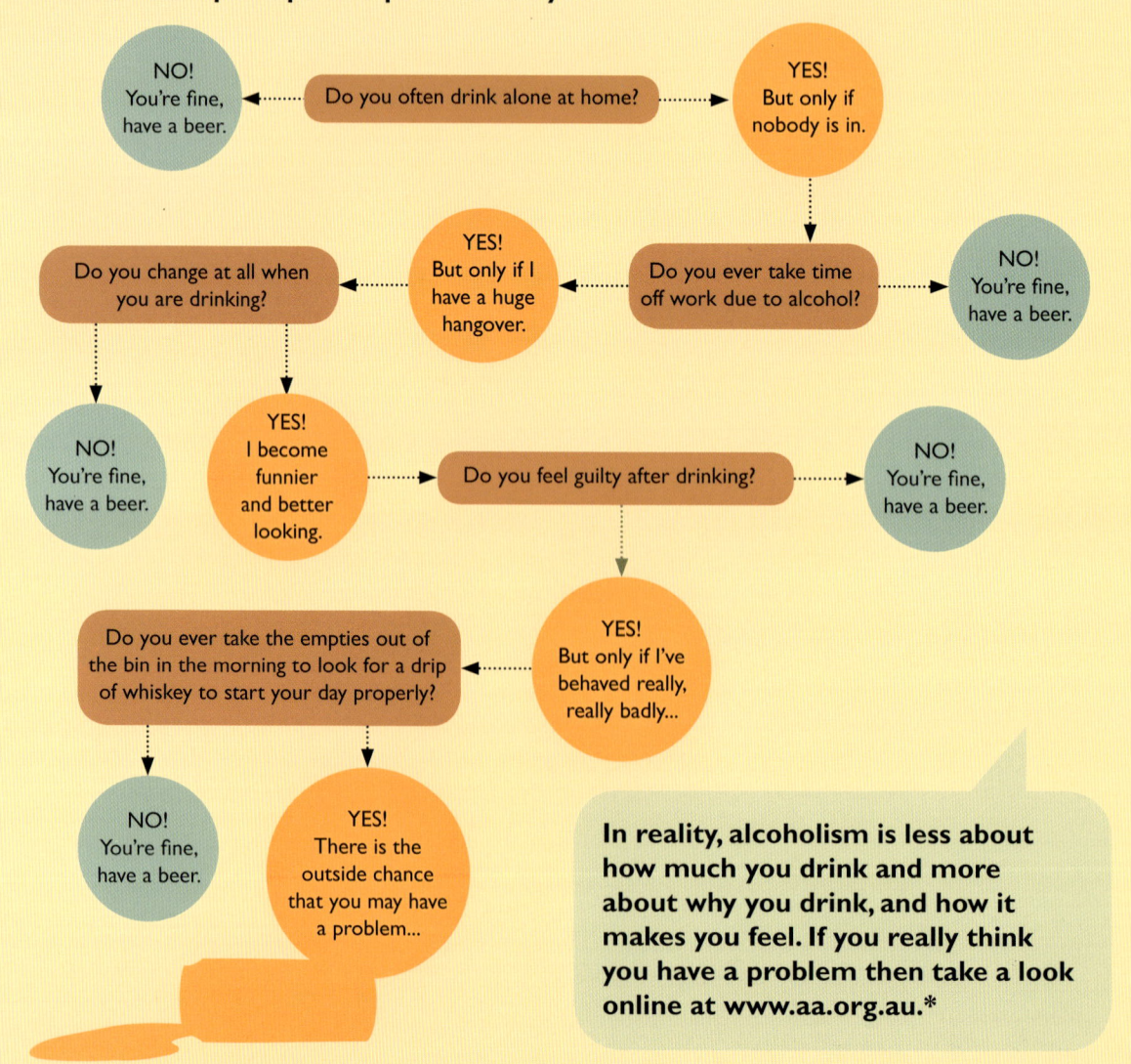

Do you often drink alone at home?
- NO! You're fine, have a beer.
- YES! But only if nobody is in. → **Do you ever take time off work due to alcohol?**
  - NO! You're fine, have a beer.
  - YES! But only if I have a huge hangover. → **Do you change at all when you are drinking?**
    - NO! You're fine, have a beer.
    - YES! I become funnier and better looking. → **Do you feel guilty after drinking?**
      - NO! You're fine, have a beer.
      - YES! But only if I've behaved really, really badly... → **Do you ever take the empties out of the bin in the morning to look for a drip of whiskey to start your day properly?**
        - NO! You're fine, have a beer.
        - YES! There is the outside chance that you may have a problem...

In reality, alcoholism is less about how much you drink and more about why you drink, and how it makes you feel. If you really think you have a problem then take a look online at www.aa.org.au.*

*Apologies for the serious and sudden break from flippant humour with this information, it will not be repeated again.

Dr Google

Worried about minor ailments? Why go to a health professional when you can work yourself into a panic attack in less than two hours of obsessively searching Google? 'Lupus, is it lupus?!'

SYMPTOMS	WHAT YOU THINK IT IS	WHAT IT PROBABLY IS	TREATMENT*
Short of breath after walking up stairs.	Heart attack warning signs.	You're unfit.	It probably is a warning sign, but a very early one – like 30 years in advance. Just shift some weight and exercise.
Recurring headaches.	Brain tumour.	Recurring headaches.	Take some Panadol, drink more water. Get it checked out if it continues for too long.
Bloated & painful stomach.	Stomach cancer.	Stomach ache.	Drink more water, eat more veg and stay off curry and wine for at least a day or two.
Blood on toilet paper.	Bowel cancer.	Haemorrhoids.	Drink more water, eat more veg, get some ointment. See the doc if it persists and they'll send a camera up.
Heaviness in testicles.	Testicular cancer.	Probably need a wank.	Have a wank.
Nasty red & brown lump on neck.	No idea.	No idea.	Sounds pretty bad. Don't want to worry you, but you should really get that checked out as soon as possible.
Excessive worry about physical symptoms.	Hypochondria	It's very common for blokes to worry about this.	Pull yourself together, go and see the doctor, stay off Google for at least the next 24 hours.

For many men, the table above could stretch to 20 pages and include anything from suspected irregular heartbeat to premature Alzheimer's. Remember, the medical centre is your friend.

*Ignore author's advice and visit the doctor in all cases. The book advance certainly wouldn't stretch to a legal case.

Sick Roadmap

Despite the flippant way health has been treated in this book so far, there is every chance that you will suffer from various ailments as your years advance. Here is a handy checklist to fuel your insomnia.

20s: Mostly just hangovers, footy injuries and an STD if you're not careful. Eat what you want, have the odd cigarette, ride a motorbike and worry about it all later.

30s: Time to start looking at blood pressure, cholesterol, blood sugars and all that. Give up smoking by now and cut down on the grog a bit.

40s: You'll have an ECG and colonoscopy if you haven't already as a result of Dr Google. Might have a knee replacement, and you'll give an involuntary groan when rising from armchairs.

50s: The doctor will definitely go rectal if he hasn't already. And forget the knee replacement, you're in hip replacement territory. You'll be on first-name terms with the doc.

60+: If you've made it this far then go for your life! Bound to be the odd 'procedure' and heart scare, but at least you can turn down the hearing aid and ignore everyone.

While this might all seem quite confronting, when celebrities die in their 60s people tend to say 'He wasn't that old, either'; strangely, many men tend to find this statement quite reassuring.

Dentist No-Go

MAN vs LIFE

The graph that represents dentist appointment attendance is every bit as harsh as an injection with a big needle into your soft, fleshy gums. Hopefully sentences such as this do not prolong your absence.

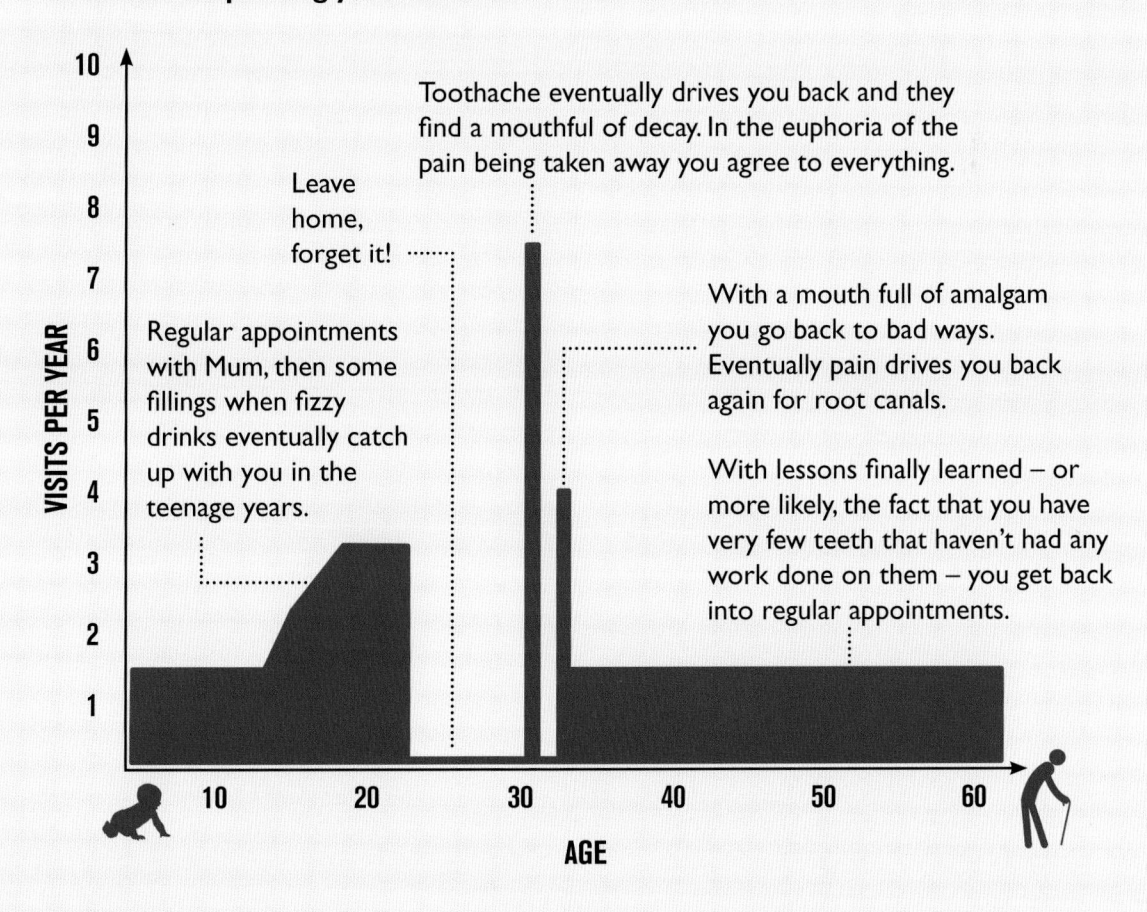

VISITS PER YEAR (y-axis: 1–10)
AGE (x-axis: 10–60)

- Regular appointments with Mum, then some fillings when fizzy drinks eventually catch up with you in the teenage years.
- Leave home, forget it!
- Toothache eventually drives you back and they find a mouthful of decay. In the euphoria of the pain being taken away you agree to everything.
- With a mouth full of amalgam you go back to bad ways. Eventually pain drives you back again for root canals.
- With lessons finally learned – or more likely, the fact that you have very few teeth that haven't had any work done on them – you get back into regular appointments.

Whether it's pain or finance keeping you away, make an appointment. Then cancel at the last minute, claiming you're working interstate.*

*Note to the author's dentist: this is clearly meant as a joke, and is not something he would endorse. He really was in Adelaide last week.

Mental Health

No matter how stable the majority of men might seem, the chances are that all men will suffer from mental illness at some point in their life. Conditions such as selective mutism (especially when reading the paper) can kick in as early as the mid teens.

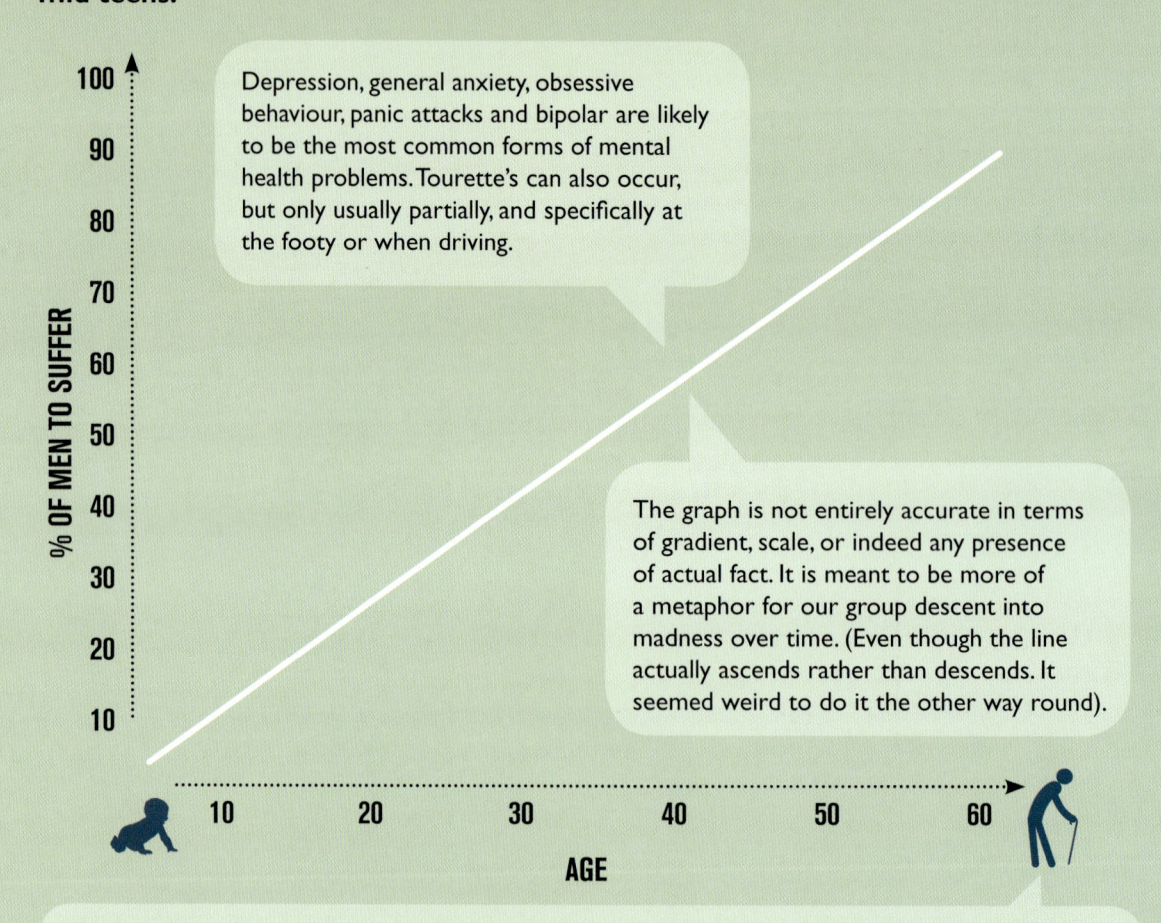

> Depression, general anxiety, obsessive behaviour, panic attacks and bipolar are likely to be the most common forms of mental health problems. Tourette's can also occur, but only usually partially, and specifically at the footy or when driving.

> The graph is not entirely accurate in terms of gradient, scale, or indeed any presence of actual fact. It is meant to be more of a metaphor for our group descent into madness over time. (Even though the line actually ascends rather than descends. It seemed weird to do it the other way round).

% OF MEN TO SUFFER vs *AGE*

Rather like the page on alcohol (page 54), there is a certain reticence to be glib about this area of a man's life. Having said that, if you've reached page 60 of this book and still think it may provide real answers to your problems, then you really do need clinical help.

Spirituality*

Most men of our age will feel slightly uncomfortable around use of the word God with any lack of irony, and will point to science for all the answers. Despite that, we can't help feeling that religious people are more content than us. And spiritual people even more so.

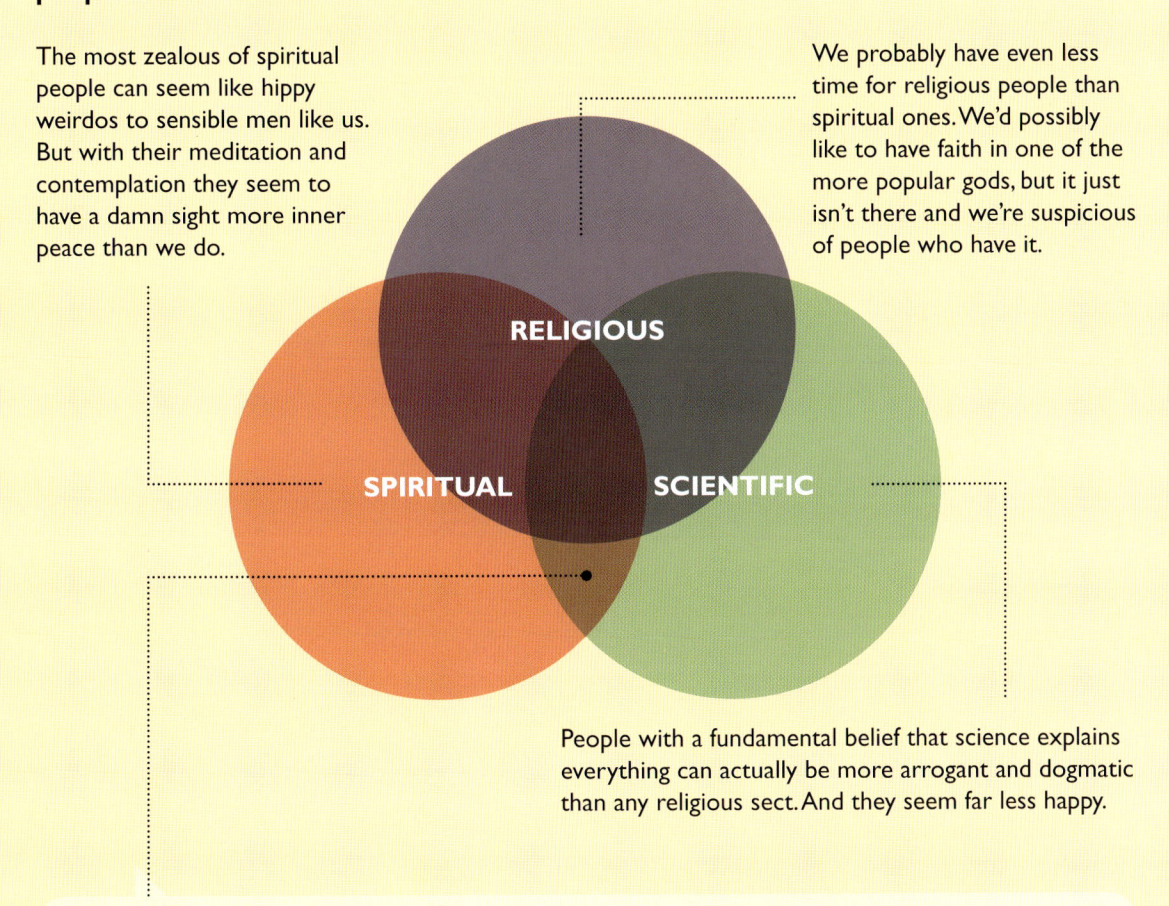

The most zealous of spiritual people can seem like hippy weirdos to sensible men like us. But with their meditation and contemplation they seem to have a damn sight more inner peace than we do.

We probably have even less time for religious people than spiritual ones. We'd possibly like to have faith in one of the more popular gods, but it just isn't there and we're suspicious of people who have it.

RELIGIOUS

SPIRITUAL   **SCIENTIFIC**

People with a fundamental belief that science explains everything can actually be more arrogant and dogmatic than any religious sect. And they seem far less happy.

For the record, the author sits around here: with belief in a universal intelligence that underpins the universe, providing natural order; and a life force that exists in everything, and which provides the spiritual link between mind and body. Okay, back to the humour now.

*Worth giving this some thought. If you feel unhappy at your core, then no big TV or new car is going to solve it.

Sex & Relationships

63 Love/Sex/Friendship Zones
64 Wife Mapping
65 Sex/Masturbation Frequency
66 Sex/Masturbation Venues
67 Getting Sex
68 Man vs Venus
69 Marriage Problems
70 The Divorce Gap
71 Worlds Collide

Love/Sex/Friendship Zones

Juggling love, sex and friendship within a relationship is every bit as precarious as the circus performer keeping his chainsaw, bowling ball and flaming torch in the air at once. And sadly over time those Big Hairy Audacious Goals for your sex life turn into Low Hanging Fruit...

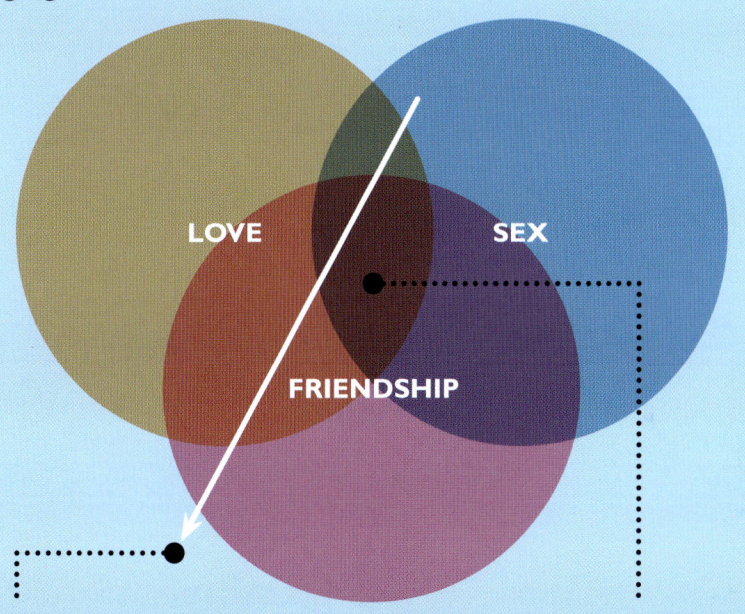

LOVE **SEX**

FRIENDSHIP

The arrow reflects the trajectory of a typical relationship. Purely sex at the start, then love as well, then the holy trinity. As sex starts to slow up, the relationship passes into love and friendship. If it reaches purely friendship or heads outside the circles then an exit strategy is near.

Rather like the Bermuda Triangle, this three-sided area is slightly ethereal. Some people get lost in it, but others simply do not believe it exists. (NB: When we talk about being in the Love / Friendship Zone, we are not saying that sex does not happen, but that it is no longer a driving force in the relationship).

Some married men* would like to stay in the Love/Friendship Zone for ever, but reach an agreement with their wives to supplement their sex life with various young porn stars (like the dad in *Seventh Heaven* meets Charlie Sheen). This is unlikely to be achieved and is certainly a difficult, robust conversation to initiate.

*Clearly the author disassociates himself from this sort of thinking, as do any of his close friends or colleagues.

Wife Mapping

Marriage is for life; unless you get a divorce, like one in three people. You still need to be very careful around the criteria you apply, however, when considering the correct strategic fit in any spousal mergers.

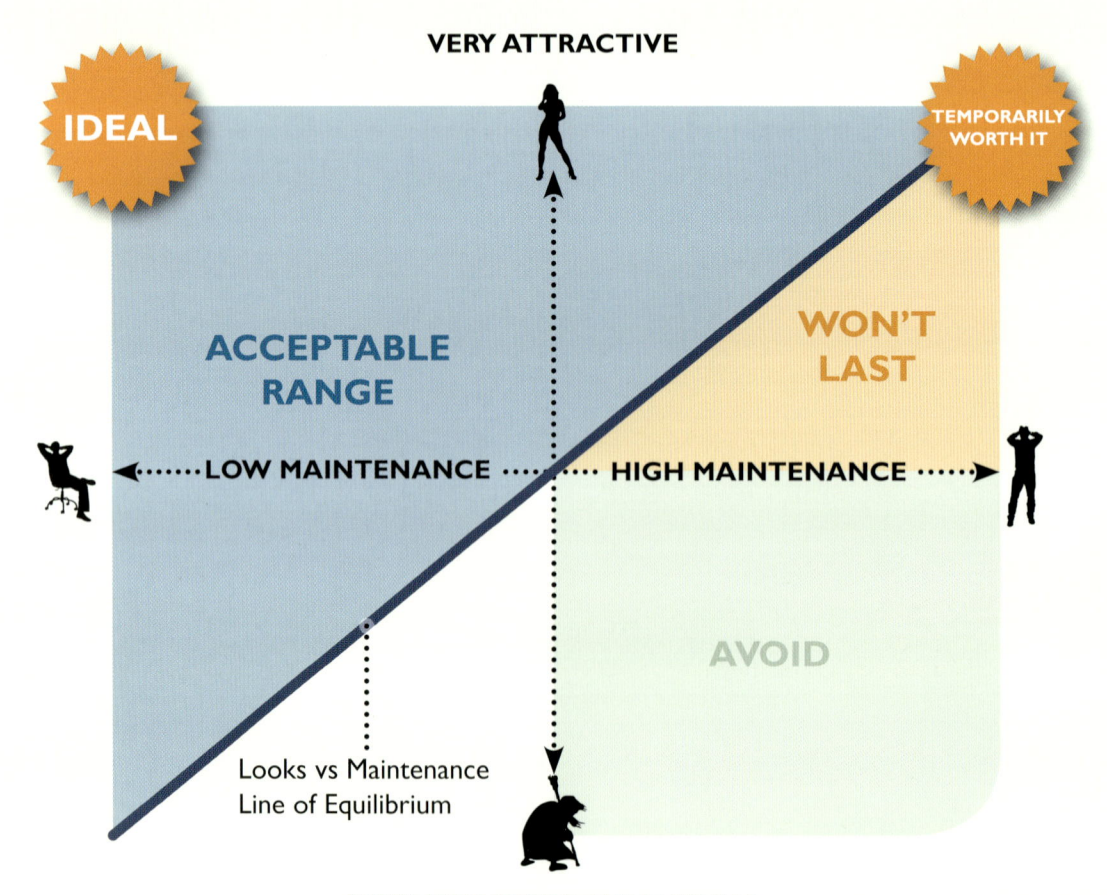

VERY ATTRACTIVE

IDEAL

TEMPORARILY WORTH IT

ACCEPTABLE RANGE

WON'T LAST

← ····· LOW MAINTENANCE ····· • ····· HIGH MAINTENANCE ····· →

AVOID

Looks vs Maintenance Line of Equilibrium

NOT VERY ATTRACTIVE AT ALL

Remember, the beauty of a potential partner at 25 may not always be sustainable. Analyse their mum's looks, and note that women with darker hair and skin tend to age better than pale, blonde ones.*

*No scientific proof to this, it's just a theory, really, on the part of the author – who, ironically, is pale and blonde.

Sex/Masturbation Frequency

MAN vs LIFE

The graphs below are a typical example of how a married man's frequency of having sex (either in collaboration with a partner, or as a sole pursuit) varies across time and circumstance.

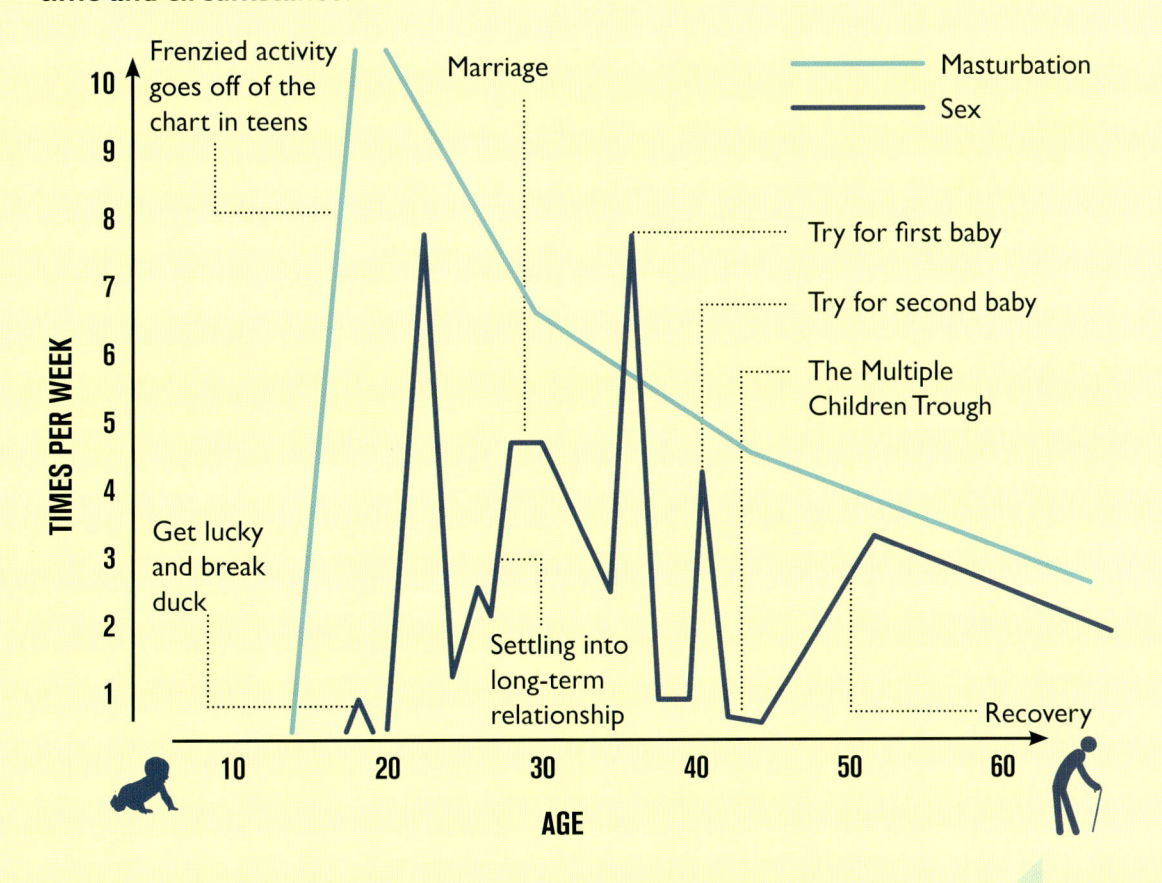

TIMES PER WEEK (vertical axis: 1–10)
AGE (horizontal axis: 10–60)

Legend:
- Masturbation
- Sex

Annotations:
- Frenzied activity goes off of the chart in teens
- Get lucky and break duck
- Marriage
- Settling into long-term relationship
- Try for first baby
- Try for second baby
- The Multiple Children Trough
- Recovery

While the sex graph shows volatility throughout a man's life, our trusty friend masturbation has a much more predictable path. There is also largely a lack of causality between the two: most men see masturbation as not so much an alternative to sex, but an alternative to, say, reading or watching TV (or indeed in some cases an accompaniment). It's just something to do because you can.

Sex/Masturbation Venues

While more adventurous in youth, the venues for sex becomes less spontaneous in marriage – especially after a family emerges. Below are listed the typical place that our man has sex or masturbates.

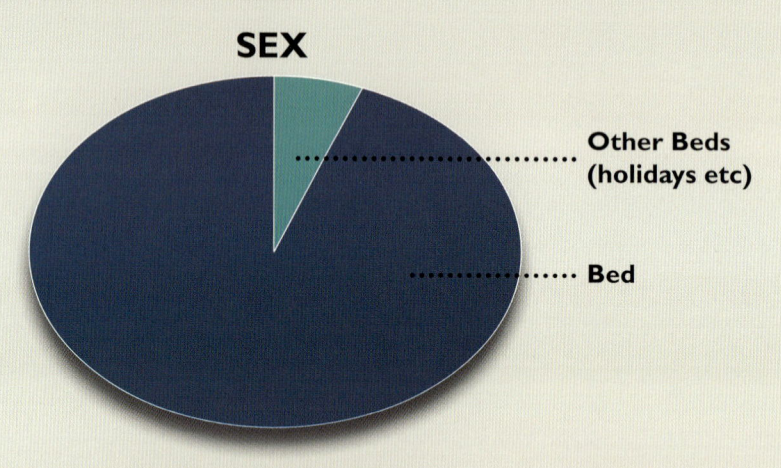

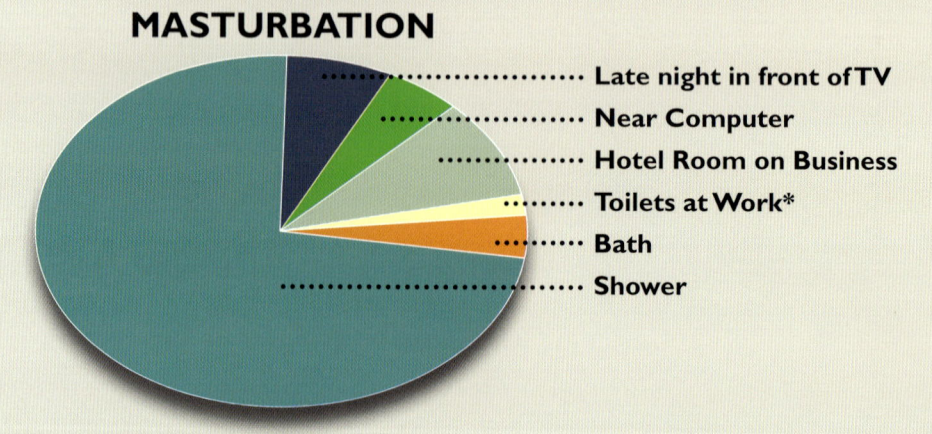

SEX

- Other Beds (holidays etc)
- Bed

MASTURBATION

- Late night in front of TV
- Near Computer
- Hotel Room on Business
- Toilets at Work*
- Bath
- Shower

The only conclusion that can be formed is that for our demographic of 35+, the men are making more of an effort to vary their masturbation life than they are to bring variety to their actual sex life.

*The author would like to reassure his current employers that this is not something he has done for a number of years.

Getting Sex

The key issue with initiating sex is not to be too obvious with your strategy. A bit like the child's game *What's the Time, Mr Wolf?*, you have to creep up a step at a time without being noticed, until you're almost on top of them. And there is the chance you'll be busted at any time.

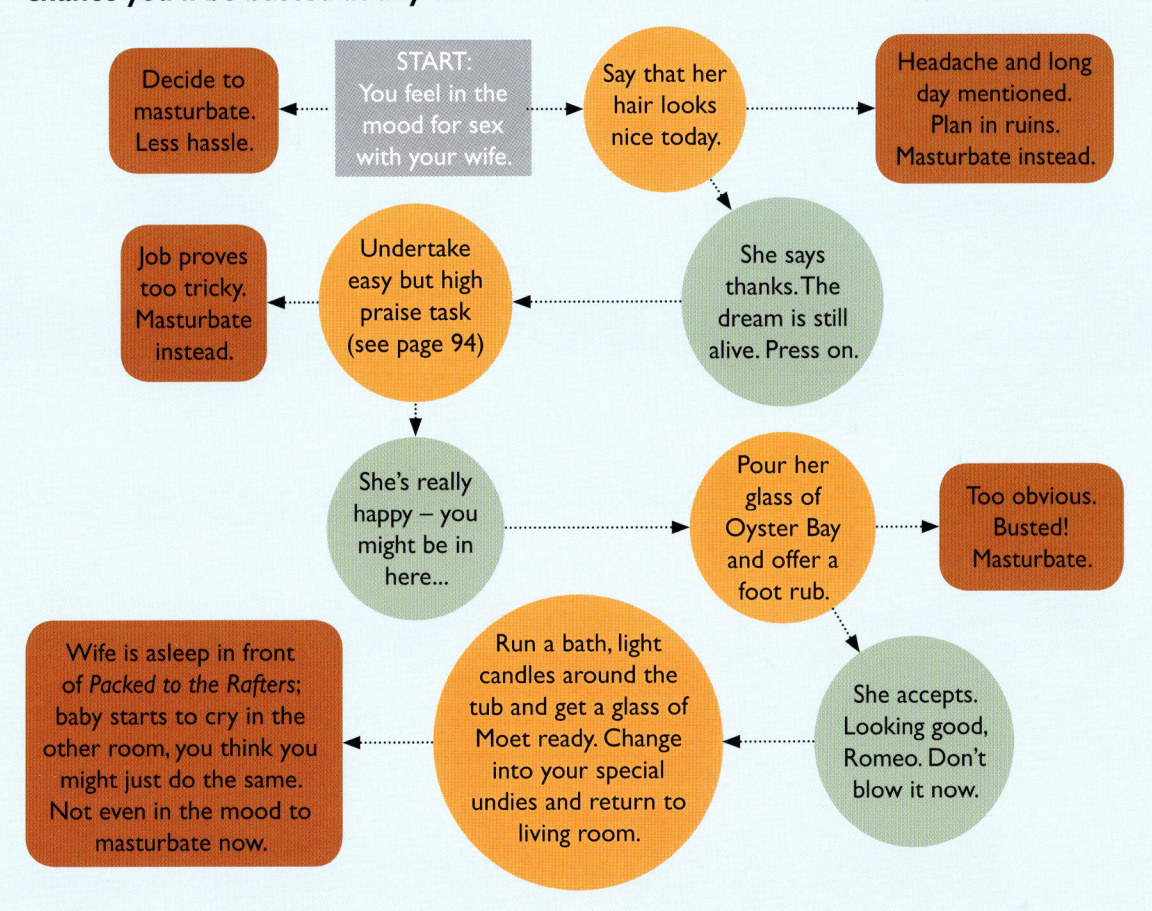

- **Decide to masturbate. Less hassle.**
- **START: You feel in the mood for sex with your wife.**
- **Say that her hair looks nice today.**
- **Headache and long day mentioned. Plan in ruins. Masturbate instead.**
- **Job proves too tricky. Masturbate instead.**
- **Undertake easy but high praise task (see page 94)**
- **She says thanks. The dream is still alive. Press on.**
- **She's really happy – you might be in here...**
- **Pour her glass of Oyster Bay and offer a foot rub.**
- **Too obvious. Busted! Masturbate.**
- **Wife is asleep in front of *Packed to the Rafters*; baby starts to cry in the other room, you think you might just do the same. Not even in the mood to masturbate now.**
- **Run a bath, light candles around the tub and get a glass of Moet ready. Change into your special undies and return to living room.**
- **She accepts. Looking good, Romeo. Don't blow it now.**

It's important to know intuitively when the whole process has broken down without that fact being verbalised. No point continuing with a failing strategy, and missing the footy or a curry, only to be denied at the final hurdle.

Man vs Venus

It's amazing that men and women stay together for a month or two, let alone years on end, when you consider the lack of strategic fit. Harsh though it may sound it ultimately comes down to an internal negotiation with regard to a) Your continued desire to have sex with a partner, b) How entangled financial and parental circumstances are, and c) How happy you are with family life in general versus how much you can put up with all of the differences (some listed below):

♀ Women like 'doing things' and men don't like 'doing things'. As soon as a wife starts saying 'I thought it would be nice for us all to...' you feel yourself tense up. School concerts, BBQs with other parents, firework displays... we subconsciously sulk or pick fights to get out of this stuff. We'd have rather sat on the sofa and watched our own wedding on TV than actually attend, if that had indeed been possible.

♀ Women like their friends' children, men are only interested in their own ones. In fact, we can hardly remember the names of some of the others.

♀ Women leave the toilet seat down all the time, so we end up urinating on it in the middle of the night. Amazing that this is seen the other way round by females.

♂ Men are good at flicking TV channels; we almost have a sixth sense of what is on a channel without stopping on it.

♂ Men will eat food off other people's plates. 'Are you going to leave that?' is a phrase men are happy to use. We will even eat food off the floor if we think it's been there for less than 24 hours.

♂ Men are good at map reading and have a good sense of direction. We often display this by screeching to a halt and snatching the A–Z out of our wife's hands, saying 'Here, let me have that...'

♀ Women have lots of friends that they do lots of different things with – many of which don't involve alcohol. Men have two or three friends and they meet them at the pub. Or play sport, then go to the pub.

This list hardly scratches the surface, but does begin to build a picture of the incompatibility and lack of synergy – the sheer diversity – between the two sexes. Opposites clearly do attract. At least for a while...

Marriage Problems

Let's ignore the big ticket items: affairs, domestic violence, fertility issues; solving these problems is well beyond the scope of this book. We'll concentrate instead on more of the funny, irritating stuff for our next table.

Problem	Reason for annoyance	Do you do it yourself?	Solution
Leaving the kitchen bin overflowing.	Sticking fingers in BBQ sauce when binning a teabag.	No, you empty it when it's 80% full.	Moan about it every time it happens for about seven or eight years, until change slowly starts to take place.
No towels left in the bathroom.	Needing to walk naked and wet to linen cupboard.	Not sure. Possibly. That's not the point...	When your wife's book club is round, stomp naked and dripping wet into the lounge asking where the towels are...
Putting dishes in the sink and leaving them.	Sometimes have to empty the sink and start again.	Again, that's not the point.	Say sarcastically: 'Did you expect these to wash themselves?' To which you get the response: 'They're just soaking...'
Driving a different way around car park.	Bit unsettling. You normally go up and then left.	Clearly not. It's always quieter the way you go.	Tut loudly and ask why we always go this way when it's better the other way. Response: 'I prefer this way...' Tut again.
Wife coming home slightly tipsy.	Ambience of quiet night in front of TV ruined.	No. You come home smashed when she's in bed.	Take a pious approach to the situation and stupidly blow the brownie points you've just earned looking after kids.
Not in the mood for sex tonight.	You are in the mood for sex tonight.	Only if there's a footy game you can't miss.	See bespoke strategy detailed on page 67. It's worth a bash (so to speak).
Snoring.	Keeps you awake one night out of 365.	Apparently, but there's no real proof.	Wake them up to tell them they're snoring, then doze off peacefully as they're left staring at the ceiling.

While these start off as cute little idiosyncrasies in the early days, after 5–10 years and 1–3 children, they can occasionally lead to highly irrational displays of near-insane behaviour. Apparently.

The Divorce Gap

At times of extreme stress, divorce may seem like the only solution to the mental toll that your current situation is taking. This is an illusion, as life can get a whole lot worse than you think.

FEMALE

4. Wife meets bloke who is taller and slimmer than you. Kids think he's cool.

3. Wife seems happy with life and is even glad that you split up now.

2. Wife starts going to gym and doing Bikram yoga. Loses 15 kg.

1. Kids thrive under Mum's guidance in a more stable home environment.

DIVORCE

MALE

1. Kids visit your studio apartment every other Sunday and hate it.

2. You go to the pub most nights with blokes you work with. Gain 15 kg.

3. Meaningless sex with women that you hardly even like starts to erode your soul.

4. Overweight, addicted to porn, borderline drunk; you sit alone and ponder your folly.

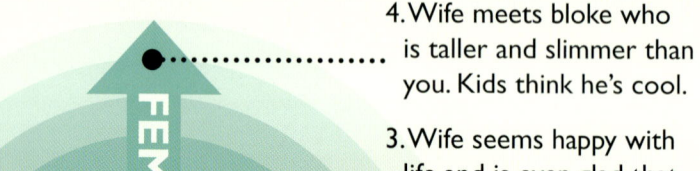

> Okay, so this is a bleak and one-sided view of what can probably be a liberating experience for both parties in some cases. It just provides food for thought before any hasty decisions are made.*

*Note to self: Haven't bought wife flowers for a while, maybe get some on the way home tonight...

Worlds Collide

Your gym buddies have been told that you were an amateur boxer as a kid, and yet your school friends remember you crying when Karen Jackson punched you for pulling her pigtails. These different sets of friends simply can't meet...

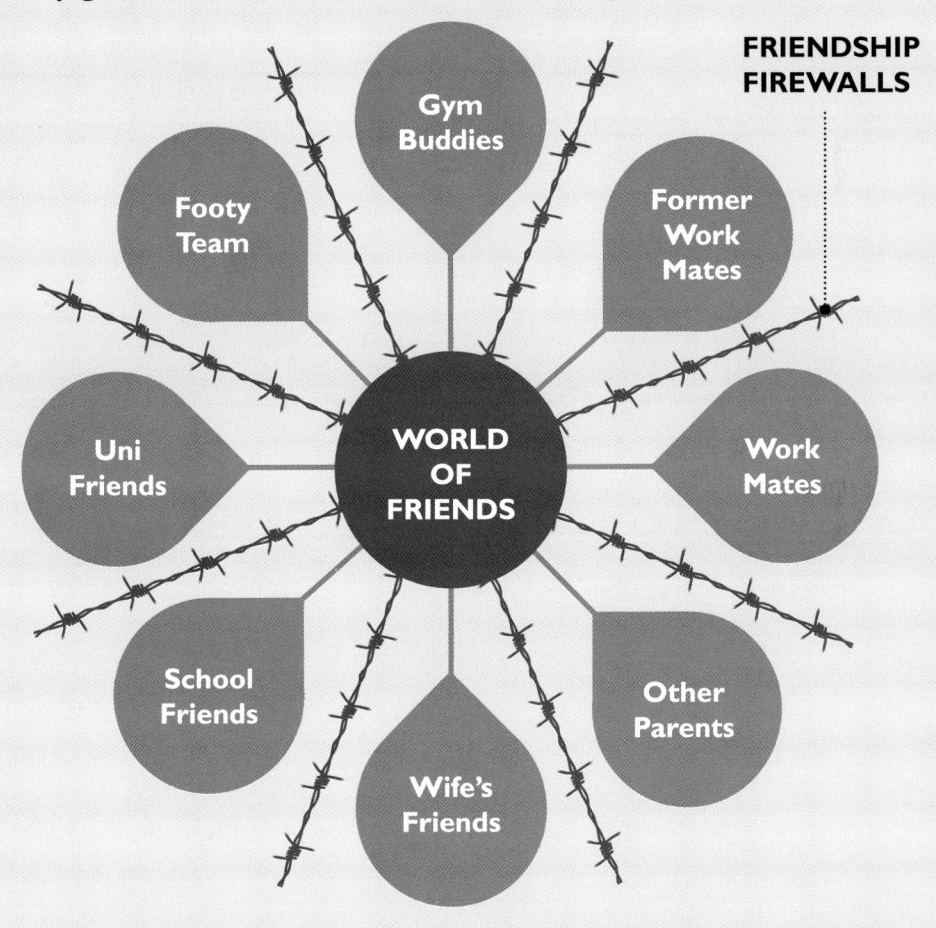

FRIENDSHIP FIREWALLS

- Gym Buddies
- Former Work Mates
- Work Mates
- Other Parents
- Wife's Friends
- School Friends
- Uni Friends
- Footy Team

WORLD OF FRIENDS

Keep those firewalls in place, so that your chameleon-like personalities and parallel pasts can be maintained. At least at 35+ you're past the weddings phase in life where worlds constantly collide.

Kids

73 Pregnancy & Birth
74 Stress Graphs
75 The Business Case
76 Baby Jobs
77 The Books Don't Say…
78 Org Charts
79 School Roadmap
80 Exxy Curricular
81 Party Mapping
82 Xmas Gift Inflation
83 Bedtime Stories

Pregnancy & Birth

MAN vs LIFE

You're having a baby, the most joyous experience that anyone can have in life. We're not here to dispute that fact, simply to add some extra colour to what you can expect when expecting.

- Doctors say the word 'vagina' fairly regularly with no hint of a giggle whatsoever. Even if you catch their eye and smirk, they refuse to have a laugh.

- The cravings thing is a bit overblown on TV; in fact, you feel a bit cheated that you don't have to dash to petrol stations at 3 am for some jellybeans.

- You proclaim that you will give up drinking for nine months as a show of solidarity with your wife. Within three weeks you are drinking for both of you.

- Those little scan pics are all the same. It isn't even your baby, it's just a generic scan that they have thousands of in a box under the ultrasound machine.*

- Sex is a bit weird when pregnant. You feel a bit uneasy about what you're going to poke. All a bit unnerving.

- In pre-natal classes all of the other expectant dads seem like dickheads; but in the Mothers' Group the dads all seem okay. So do you change, or do they change over that nine months?

- Towards the end of pregnancy a huge pillow arrangement will be put in place every night. You will be annexed to a corner of the bed, like a eunuch on the edge of a cushion-filled harem tent.

- You'll buy a name book. Josh and Jack will probably make the short list. Tell your parents Adolf and Osama are also on it, just to see their reaction.

- You'll chat about all the things you see other parents do, that you will never do with your child. Within three months you'll have done 80% of those things.

- At 37 weeks you will freak out. Really.

> If you haven't had kids then this page will not make a lot of sense. No, don't nod at the page, you really don't understand. Reread this page when you have been a parent for six months and it will hopefully resonate on a far deeper level.

*Made that bit up. But you never know...

Stress Graphs

For the first two years of childhood it sometimes feels like you're on a gruelling executive training course, held offsite, at which you also party hard – and which lasts 24/7 for more than 18 months.

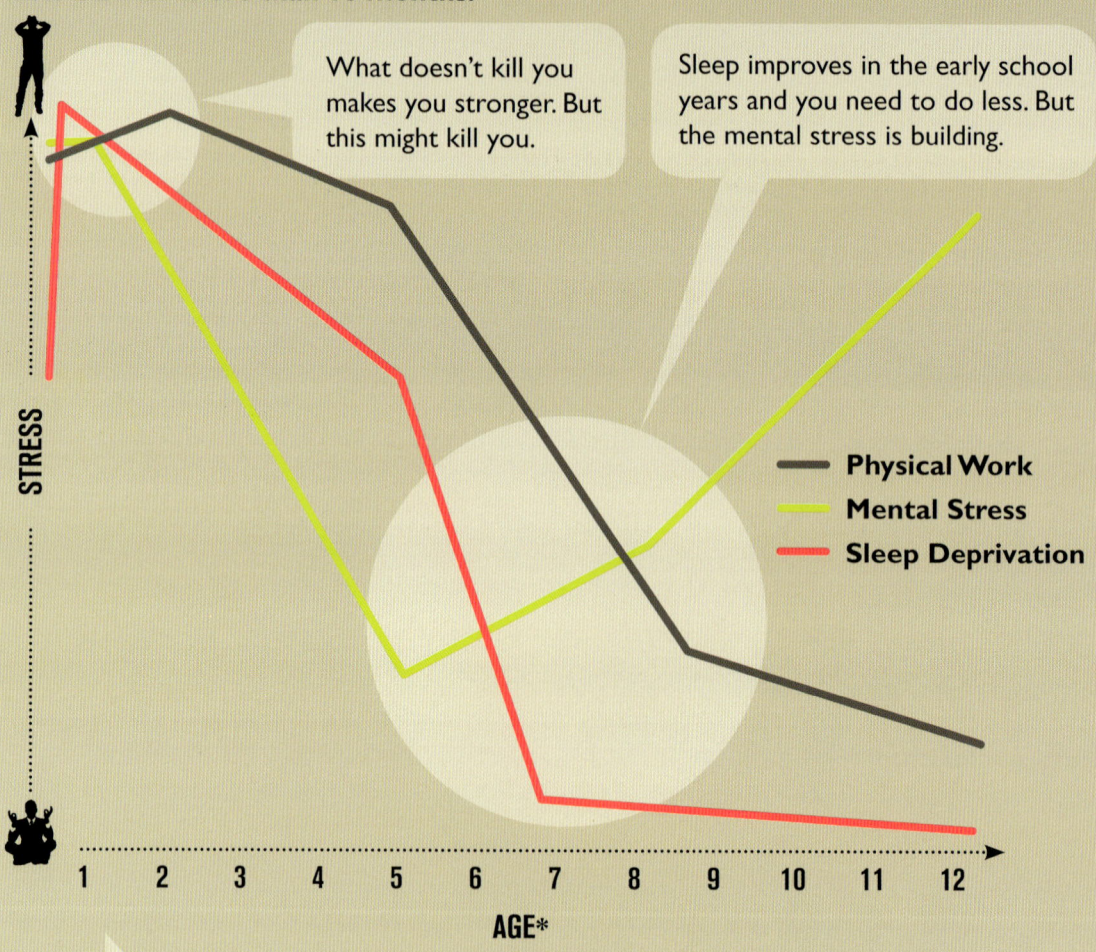

> What doesn't kill you makes you stronger. But this might kill you.

> Sleep improves in the early school years and you need to do less. But the mental stress is building.

— Physical Work
— Mental Stress
— Sleep Deprivation

STRESS

AGE*

1 2 3 4 5 6 7 8 9 10 11 12

*The graph only goes to 12, because that's how old the author's eldest child is. Other parents of teenagers indicate that it gets harder mentally: 'bloody nightmare' is the phrase most often used.

The Business Case

If having kids was purely down to a business case, then the world's population would rapidly diminish. It's not a cost-based decision by any means.

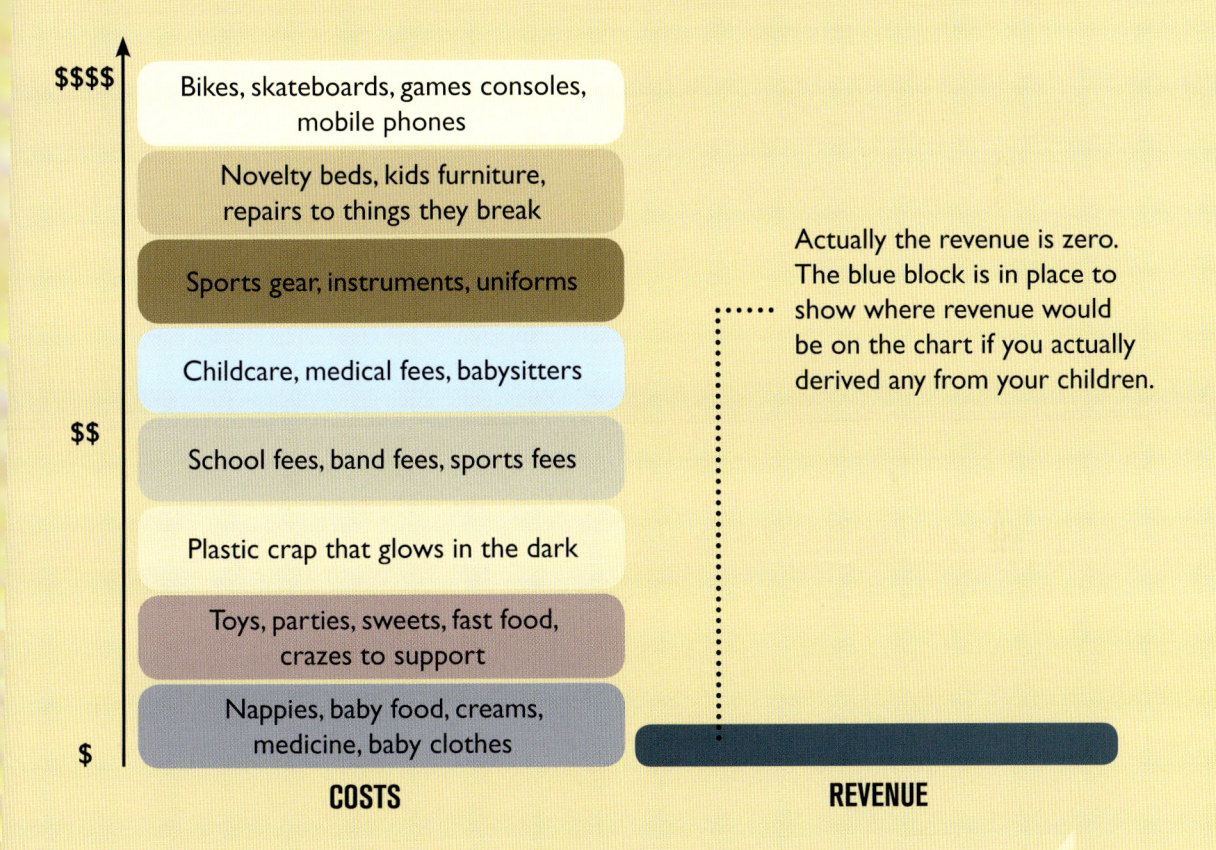

Costs (from top $$$$ to bottom $):
- Bikes, skateboards, games consoles, mobile phones
- Novelty beds, kids furniture, repairs to things they break
- Sports gear, instruments, uniforms
- Childcare, medical fees, babysitters
- School fees, band fees, sports fees
- Plastic crap that glows in the dark
- Toys, parties, sweets, fast food, crazes to support
- Nappies, baby food, creams, medicine, baby clothes

COSTS | **REVENUE**

Actually the revenue is zero. The blue block is in place to show where revenue would be on the chart if you actually derived any from your children.

The graph only includes ongoing operating costs and ignores the fixed capital costs in start-up phase: stroller, cot, bassinet, change table (what a racket that is), car seat, sling, baby bath, nappy bucket, bottles, steriliser, etc. The costs are also based on direct costs, rather than some indirect costs that can be associated with children and that are often huge – needing a bigger house, needing a bigger car, needing to live in more family-friendly environments.

Baby Jobs

You have a relatively easy role in the first year of a baby's life compared to your wife, and yet you seem to complain far more. These are the main functions that you will perform.

Changing Nappies
It's actually far easier than you'd expect – except smelly ones at 5 am with a hangover.

Doing Food Shop
Bliss – gets you out of the house for an hour.

Taking Them for a Walk
Again, it's a pretty easy gig if the sun's out and you have a three-wheel buggy.

Showing Support During the Night Feed
This involves getting up at 3 am when the baby feeds and either a) watching Jerry Springer on cable, b) twigging that there's some soccer on and making a coffee, or c) falling asleep on the sofa until you're forcibly told to go to bed.

Sterilising Bottles
Pain in the arse. Feels like you're working in a bottle plant at times. You get pretty good at it, though.

> If you have more than one child then this list becomes too complicated to even contemplate compiling.

The Books Don't Say...

Most child-related tasks and issues are covered by a range of baby books. Some things are too trivial to get a mention. Here are a few:

! Some nights you will pretend you are asleep simply to avoid dealing with your screaming child. Terrible but true.

! Controlled crying is the baby equivalent of dog years. A minute seems like an hour.

! At some point you will tread on a small toy, like a piece of Lego, in the dark of night. You will swear and swear and swear.

! You cannot arrange kids' books neatly. There is no uniformity to kids' books: some are five inches tall and three feet long; others are shaped like a regular novel, but two foot thick and made of cloth; some are an inch square; others again are the size of a fridge door, made of plywood, and squeak if you lean a piece of felt against them.

! Kids' pushchairs are harder to collapse when somebody is waiting for your parking space. Busy car park + complicated Rubik's cube-style, collapsible pushchair + bloke in ute impatiently giving you the evil eye = partially severed finger and cross Daddy.

! You will have a meningitis scare at some point in your child's life. Your child will be sick and have some sort of rash. You will consult 'the warning signs of meningitis' list stuck to the fridge. The easiest symptom to check is that 'your child will shy away from light'. You will therefore hold your six-month-old screaming baby about 3 mm from a 200-watt bulb in the kitchen and they will recoil in appropriate terror.

! Turn the baby monitor off before you argue. Your dinner guests don't want to hear that 'Yes, it is your f-ing turn, because I was up 15 f-ing times in the f-ing night, and they're not even my f-ing friends'.

! It will take you five hours – possibly across two different nights – to watch a movie on DVD when you factor in child interruptions.

! You will hate homework more than you ever did as a kid.

! Putting together bikes on Xmas Eve at 11 am when drunk is very, very hard.

Hardly scratched the surface: *Man vs Child* **to follow in 6 months.**

Org Charts

It may be wise to eschew traditional organisational structures within the family unit in favour of one that suits people (in particular, you) slightly better. Here is the paradigm shift that we are suggesting:

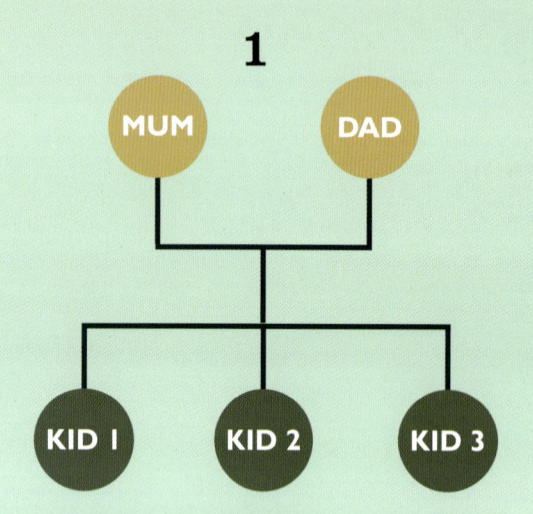

1

MUM — DAD
KID 1 — KID 2 — KID 3

Although a seemingly democratic way of doing things – egalitarian and with a flat structure – it can lead to a lack of accountability ('I thought you were doing it...'), or a shirking of responsibility ('See what your mum says...'). Kids can get a quick answer under this structure as there are two equal managers, but if they don't like the first answer they can then seek another from a different manager. No doesn't mean no.

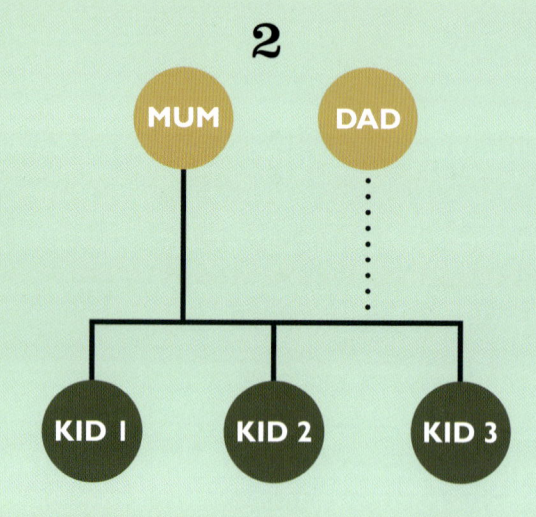

2

MUM   DAD
KID 1 — KID 2 — KID 3

This is a lot less obvious as a structure but has far clearer reporting lines. Under this structure Mum has sole responsibility for just about everything (and let's face it, she's already been acting in that role for some time). She decides on meals, schools, bed time, the lot. Dad just chips in with helpful pieces of advice – often in the most stressful of situations ('That's not how I'd have done it...').

> So as not to cause confusion under the preferred structure 2, just say 'ask your mum' to every request that comes your way.

School Roadmap

Be warned: the more you interfere in your child's education, the more you find that you need to interfere in your child's education. But here are some milestones to watch for from the sidelines.

Do you hold them back? Do you send them? They don't seem quite ready, but then again childcare is financially crippling. Send them! Biggest worry is separation anxiety. Don't worry, you'll be fine.

NAPLAN takes place in Years 3, 5 and 7. Not sure what it's really about, but there seems a lot of talk about it. Girls start to get a little bit bitchy around this time. And band starts, so get out the ear plugs.

As with previous slides, the author's eldest is still in Year 6, so has no idea what to expect at high school (public, not private). The HSC years sound horrendous by all accounts, though.

K 1 2 3 4 5 6 7 8 9 10 11 12

The novelty of uniform is starting to wear a bit thin – especially when it's lost or covered in paint. Homework is already more full-on than you remember as a 6-year-old. You start to see how bright they are – or not.

The really rich kids leave for private schools now and everyone else worries about the public/private high school dilemma. Birthday parties get more elaborate and school trips involve sleepovers.

Apart from bullying, which can be a genuinely nasty experience, what's the worst that can happen? These days qualifications aren't everything; as long as kids are happy they'll be fine. We turned out okay, didn't we? (Perhaps not, if this book is anything to go by.)

Exxy Curricular

While you definitely want the most rounded education for your child, one that goes way beyond the confines of academic study, it's gutting to shell out thousands for an instrument that will drive you up the wall.

ACTIVITY	COST	SOS SIZZLE?	TIME INVOLVED	OVERVIEW
Nippers	$	👍	Summer Saturday mornings at the beach.	You can get a coffee and a sausage sizzle and spend the morning at the beach – what else would you do?
Drama	$	👎	School lunchtime. Have to attend the odd show.	Concerts can be excruciating – especially if there are pushy mums. But it takes up little time.
Netball	$	👍	Winter Saturday mornings and evening training.	Very early starts, in cold/wet weather. Always a coffee and a snag nearby, though. Gets pretty emotional at times.
Little A's	$$	👍	Summer Saturday mornings and evening training.	Very early starts, but in good weather. Always a coffee and a snag nearby and a very relaxed vibe.
Band*	$$$	👎	Mornings, after school, concerts, neverending...	Possibly nothing as rewarding to take part in, possibly nothing as expensive and time consuming. And loud.
Chess	$	👎	After school for one evening at most.	Cheap, silent and effortless. You have to play the odd game and be beaten by 7-year-olds, but apart from that...
Soccer/ Footy etc	$	👍	Winter Saturday mornings and evening training.	Very early starts, often in wet weather. Always a coffee and a snag nearby, though. Gets pretty rough at times.

*If doing band, try and guide your child towards instruments that could play a part in their adult life (eg guitar, drums, keyboard, etc). Nobody ever whips out a violin or tuba at a party and plays *Stairway to Heaven*. Drums are also great fun for you to have a bash on when the kids are out.

Party Mapping

They are meant to be joyous expressions of love to celebrate the passing of another year in your child's life. They can actually be more stressful than childbirth itself.

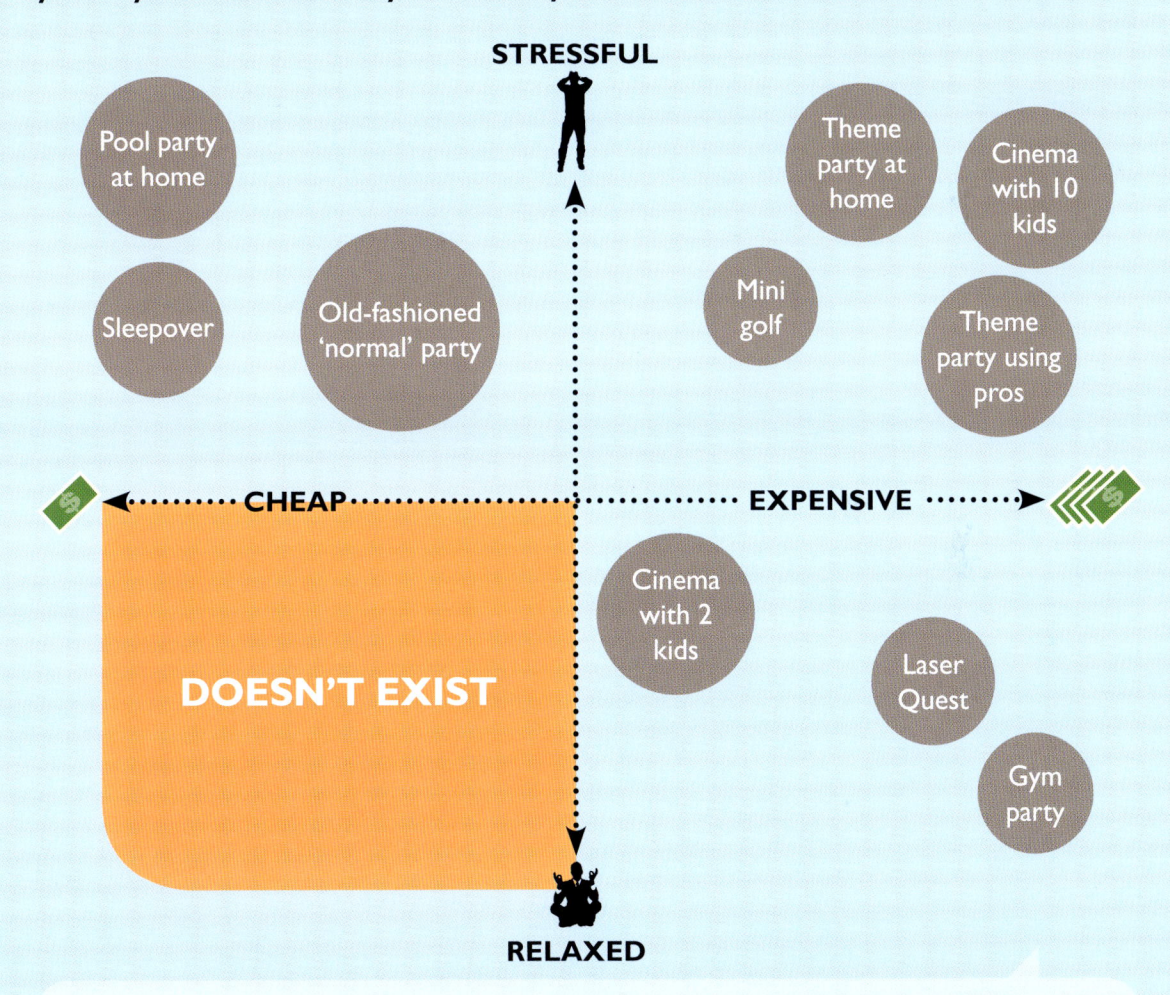

STRESSFUL

- Pool party at home
- Sleepover
- Old-fashioned 'normal' party
- Theme party at home
- Cinema with 10 kids
- Mini golf
- Theme party using pros

CHEAP ← → **EXPENSIVE**

- Cinema with 2 kids
- Laser Quest
- Gym party

DOESN'T EXIST

RELAXED

On a personal note, if the author had a dollar for every time he used the phrase 'We're not doing this again next year' at his son's last party, then he would no longer need gainful employment. For the record, we did cinema with 10 kids followed by a sleepover.

Xmas Gift Inflation

Kids start making lists to Santa around the age of 3 or 4; until then they're pretty much happy with whatever you get them. Or rather they're happy with whatever Santa brings them.*

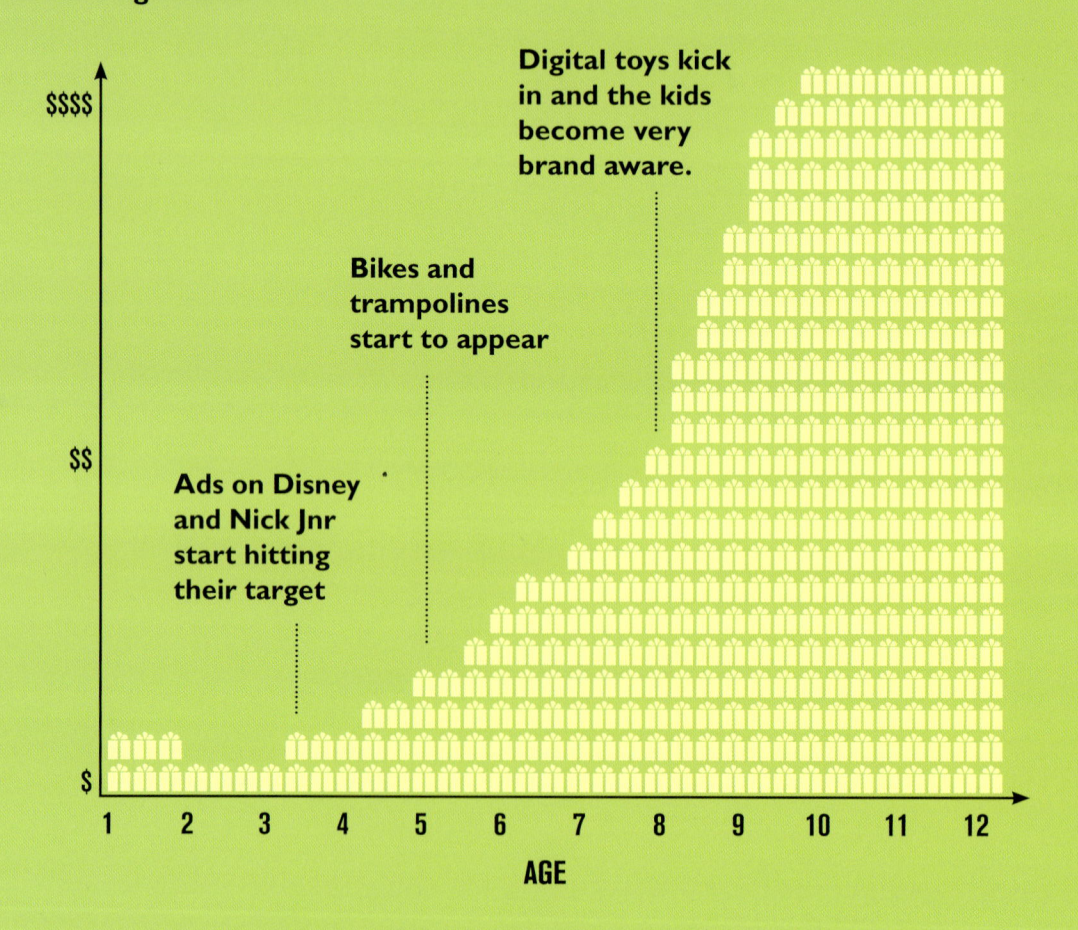

Digital toys kick in and the kids become very brand aware.

Bikes and trampolines start to appear

Ads on Disney and Nick Jnr start hitting their target

AGE: 1 2 3 4 5 6 7 8 9 10 11 12

The benefits of a **DS** or an **Xbox** over a bike or trampoline are that a) they're easier to hide, b) they're easier to wrap, and c) you don't have to put them together for hours, late on a sweaty **Xmas Eve**.

*How annoying that you don't even get credit for the expense you go to in the first 7–10 years.

Bedtime Stories

MAN vs LIFE

Fairytales all have a strong moral to them, and the moral that our kids learn is that they need to go to sleep quickly, so that they don't get to hear the full horror of the story unfold.

	SYNOPSIS	MORAL
Goldilocks & the Three Bears	High-maintenance blonde girl breaks into empty house, eats all the food, sleeps in all the beds, breaks some furniture, then escapes through a window when wild bears find her.	Don't fall asleep when doing a burglary.
The Princess & the Pea	Another high-maintenance blonde is invited to stay at castle. She relentlessly complains about a perfectly good bed and needs like 20 mattresses, because of a pea underneath.	Don't date blonde girls (see above).
The Three Little Pigs	Wolf relentlessly stalks three brothers. They're not even safe in their homes. He eats two of them, but the last one survives by boiling him alive in scalding water.	Only one way to deal with stalkers.
Hansel & Gretel	My personal favourite. Possibly in therapy, the first thing they should ask adults is 'Did you read *Hansel & Gretel* as a child?' So, husband marries second wife and step-mum doesn't want his kids. So they leave them in the woods. Just leave them. Kids find a way out of a massively frightening situation, so they take them back again. Eventually a cannibal ('What's a cannibal, Dad?'), takes them in and feeds them up ready to eat them. They escape by murdering her – burning her alive, in fact. But before they run off, they ransack her house. On escaping the woods, they bump into Dad again; the wife's left him, so he's at a loose end. He hasn't bothered to go looking for the kids, but they turn up with loads of gold and tales of murder so he takes them back. And they all lived happily ever after. Yeah, right.	Moral? Where do you start? Step-mums are evil (see also *Cinderella*, etc); fathers are fickle (see elsewhere in this book); don't just kill cannibals, rob them too. So many good messages before bed.

This is not to mention titles such as *The Goat-Faced Girl* and *The Girl without Hands*. Might as well just read some of *The Girl with the Dragon Tattoo* to send them off to dreamland.

Career & Finance

85 Disposable Income
86 Job History
87 Daily Intensity
88 Taking a Sickie
89 Work Toilets Stress
90 Sea Changes?
91 Mortgage Stress

Disposable Income

Your first weekly pay packet comes as cash (notes **AND** coins) in a little envelope. It is a beautiful, exciting thing full of promise. Twenty years later you lurch towards each monthly electronic transfer into your bank account like a drowning man trying to reach dry land.

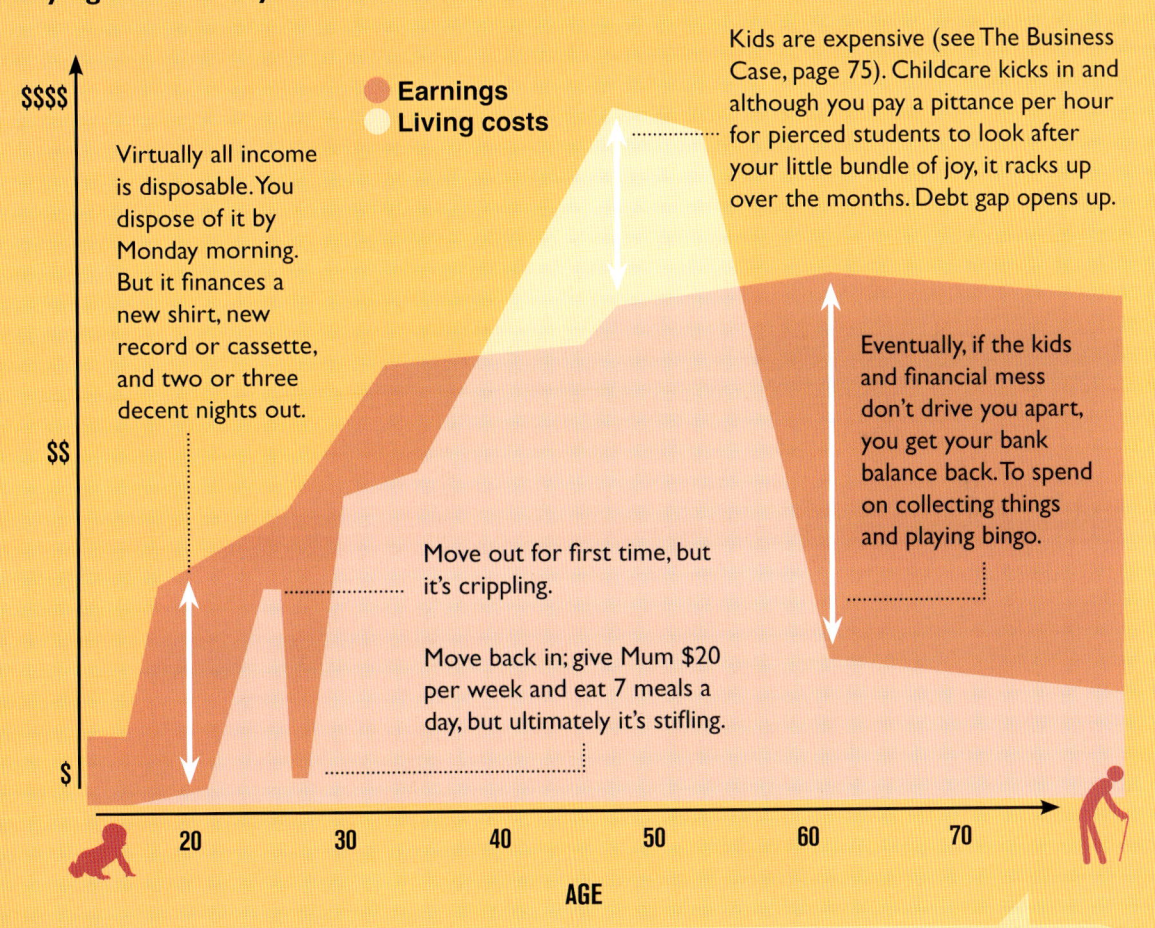

● Earnings
○ Living costs

Virtually all income is disposable. You dispose of it by Monday morning. But it finances a new shirt, new record or cassette, and two or three decent nights out.

Move out for first time, but it's crippling.

Move back in; give Mum $20 per week and eat 7 meals a day, but ultimately it's stifling.

Kids are expensive (see The Business Case, page 75). Childcare kicks in and although you pay a pittance per hour for pierced students to look after your little bundle of joy, it racks up over the months. Debt gap opens up.

Eventually, if the kids and financial mess don't drive you apart, you get your bank balance back. To spend on collecting things and playing bingo.

AGE

Mortgage payments, car loan, life insurance, medical cover, house insurance, car insurance, rego, phone, broadband, mobiles, cable TV, gym, school... hardly leaves enough for decent therapy.

Job History

Career paths differ to our parents. The author's father had two jobs and the second lasted over 30 years; the author has had 22 jobs in the last 27 years — here are seven that typify his working life. And maybe yours.

JOB	PAY	FUN?	LENGTH OF TIME	OVERVIEW
Saturdays in a big local bike shop	💵	😊😊	Sacked after 6 months for riding BMX round shop when it was empty.	The only time in whole career that it was compulsory to wear a tie. The pay was poor, but 27 years later the misappropriated supply of bicycle repair kits have still not run out.
Temporary work in an old people's home		☹☹☹	Lasted 45 minutes.	Aged 17, sent by the temp agency with no idea what to expect: the caretaker made me a cup of tea and asked what I was like with dead bodies. I was out of there before you could say 'rigor mortis'.
Potato picking in the holidays	💵	☹	Managed to stick it out for 2 weeks.	Absolutely exhausting. Like 8 hours a day of manual Tetris. Sleep was difficult due to backache and dreams of a never-ending conveyer belt of potatoes that I could never begin to finish sorting.
Behind the bar at uni	💵	😊😊😊	Four nights a week for all three years of my Uni degree.	It's amazing how much girls like you when you're still sober at 11 pm and handing them cheap vodka. Would still be working there now if it could support a mortgage and three kids.
First full-time creative role	💵	😊😊😊	First proper job. Did two of the best years of my life before moving on.	Like uni but with slightly more money. Rocked up every day at 10 am in jeans, sneakers and a T-shirt. Down the pub at 6 pm on the dot. Repeat 730 times (er, that's every day for two years). Great fun.
Middle manager	💵💵	☹	Sucked it up for six years. Far better than working in an abattoir.	That time in your career where you wear slightly smarter clothes, earn slightly more, and suck up slightly more than you used to. Still, that stress-relieving red wine every night won't pay for itself...
Senior manager	💵💵	😊😊	Four surprisingly enjoyable years that flew past.	There's a tipping point where you get to start again on a new level with all your mistakes in the past and skeletons buried elsewhere. Make the most of it, it's all downhill from here.

> The main one missing is the 'start-up' that looked so exciting, but lasted a year before a partial nervous breakdown. The promise of equity in the company turned into 15-hour days and emptying the bins at night. If you can combine fun and earnings, never let it go.

Daily Intensity

Even elite athletes can't maintain intensity at all times. It's about short, sharp bursts of effective application, broken by coffee breaks, bitching and a decent look at property online.

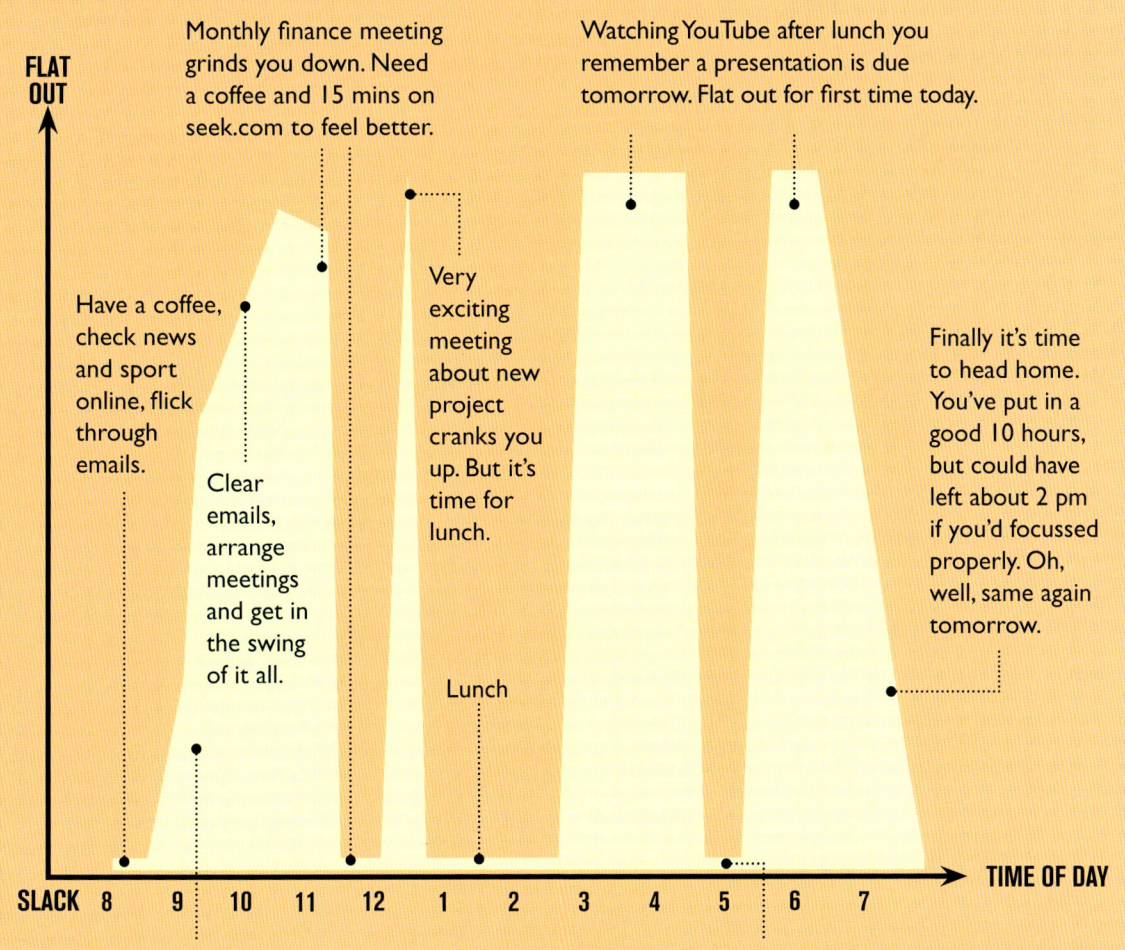

FLAT OUT

Monthly finance meeting grinds you down. Need a coffee and 15 mins on seek.com to feel better.

Watching YouTube after lunch you remember a presentation is due tomorrow. Flat out for first time today.

Have a coffee, check news and sport online, flick through emails.

Clear emails, arrange meetings and get in the swing of it all.

Very exciting meeting about new project cranks you up. But it's time for lunch.

Finally it's time to head home. You've put in a good 10 hours, but could have left about 2 pm if you'd focussed properly. Oh, well, same again tomorrow.

Lunch

SLACK 8 9 10 11 12 1 2 3 4 5 6 7   **TIME OF DAY**

You write and delete 3 snotty replies to a snotty email. Eventually you phone the guy and he apologises before you get all Tony Soprano on his arse. Adrenaline now flowing though.

Fellow manager's EA drops in for a bit of a gossip; you'd tell her you're on a deadline and can't stop to chat, but she's pretty hot so you let it go for 10 minutes.

Taking a Sickie

Nobody actually wants to waste their sick leave on being ill. You can sit at your desk coughing and spluttering; or hobble in on crutches. Sick leave is basically supplementary annual leave, isn't it?

Two Days Are Better than One

It's more believable to take two days off; with Wednesday and Thursday the best combination. Taking Mondays or Fridays off alone is suspect; while struggling in on Friday after a two-day break is admirable. It shows real commitment.

Prepare Properly in Advance

If you're taking Wednesday off, then start grumbling about your health on Tuesday. Borrow Panadol from someone loud and gossipy, preferably someone in a central role that involves communication with multiple people.

Use Facebook Wisely

Post 'Feeling really rough, need an early night' the night before. Don't post pictures of you at 2 am checked-in to the local bar.

Call Really Early and Leave Voicemail

Then back up with an email saying you tried calling earlier. Not only does it avoid a conversation, but it makes them feel guilty about getting in a bit later.

An Embarrassing Illness Prevents Further Questioning

Gastro is the obvious one. Mention you've been up on the loo all night. Nobody's going to ask: 'But was it just an ordinary bowel movement or proper diarrhoea?'

Do 'The Voice'

Even when you've actually just twisted your ankle and can't walk, you still have to do the Sick Voice. A barely audible croak, like you've been vomiting sandpaper all night. And remember to answer the phone that way all day. If they ask if they just woke you, say 'Yes, but I probably needed to try and get up anyway...'

Don't Get a Tan

Maybe sneak to the movies if you're brave, but don't lay by the pool all day. You're meant to go back paler and weaker, not looking like you've been to Bali.

Work Toilets Stress

It may be one of the most natural things to do, but a certain level of stress exists around using work toilets, particularly in the sensitive area of defecation. Here are some tips for avoiding anxiety.

1. Find a quiet toilet, well away from where you work, for number 2s. An Executive Toilet is the Holy Grail. The older, grubbier toilets nearby are fine for frequent urinal use. But you don't want to shit on your own doorstep, so to speak.

2. In a small and intimate, single-urinal, double-cubical configured toilet (one with flimsy partition walls that don't reach the floor), walk away if one of the cubicles is already occupied. It's too confronting with just a thin sheet of plywood separating you from a colleague as you each push out a stool. There might as well be a little window so that you can wave and smile weakly at each other.

3. Get in and out, with hands washed, in under 55 seconds if the coast is clear. But be wary in your haste to check for toilet paper. In the absence of loo roll, revert to newspapers if available. Bus tickets are hard to use, especially the card ones – and never try folding them to use twice. Money is an option ($50 notes can be washed afterwards), or in extreme circumstances rip up your undies and flush them away.

4. Keep your feet together, not near the bottom of the partition. In *The Shawshank Redemption*, Tim Robbins's character says, 'Nobody ever notices a man's shoes' when re-telling his escape. In the toilet cubical situation you're practically hypnotised by the glimpse of another man's footwear. Somewhere in your paranoia you believe the information that your shit stinks may be passed on to other colleagues ('Yeah, it was definitely him, I recognised the desert boots...') Never talk to somebody in the adjoining cubical, either, even if you believe you are having a seizure.

5. Never attempt the shuffle (eg grab trousers at half-mast and shuffle to the next cubicle mid-crap when you realise there's no toilet paper). Too risky. If someone walks in at that moment you have to walk straight back to your desk and type a resignation letter.

6. If someone enters the cubicle next to you, then freeze and clench. If you are already engaged, then put a wad of paper (10 handfuls) down the toilet as a landing pad. Cough in a French accent at the appropriate time and then get the hell out of there.

Sea Changes?

Assuming the audience for this book are white collar desk-jockeys with a swivel chair and mouse mat, then the scope for a sea change is more of a sideways management shift than it is becoming the author of a slightly glib but humorous novelty concept book (there's not enough money in it, for a start). Here are some options then:

INDUSTRY	PAY	COOL?	HOURS	OVERVIEW*
ACCOUNTING & FINANCE	💵💵💵💵	👎👎👎	Feels like long hours even if it actually isn't.	Traditionally the most boring of occupations and little has changed. Rewarded appropriately for the grind.
MEDIA	💵	👍👍👍	Always on call on the iPhone. Stop the press?	Newspapers, magazines, television; the glamour, the excitement, the relatively small pay packet as the trade-off.
REAL ESTATE & PROPERTY	💵💵	👍👍	Flexible. Time on the road allows for ambiguity…	'Property' sounds more palatable than 'real estate', probably due to *Grand Designs* etc. Cooler than it used to be.
SALES & MARKETING	💵💵💵	👍	Long, but lunches are still part of the gig. Just.	Call them Business Development Managers or Brand Directors, they're still flogging stuff, aren't they?
INFORMATION TECHNOLOGY	💵💵💵💵	👎👎	Likely to get a DVT on any given day.	The cutting edge of future technology and the internet sounds cool. But IBM Mainframe DB2/Cobol, not so much…
ENGINEERING & SCIENCE	💵💵	👍👍	Fairly long and often on call for emergencies.	Building things, wearing hard hats, and those big blueprint drawings; always looks cool on TV these days.
MEDICAL & HEALTHCARE	💵💵💵💵	👎	Fairly long and often on call for emergencies.	Surgeons are the heroes; anaesthetists their well-paid sidekicks; but aren't managers the bad guys in medicine?

*The author would like to apologise for upsetting virtually his whole audience in the course of a single page.

Mortgage Stress

Regarded by many as more stressful than having a child – which is a really sad thought the more you think about it. And it's even more stressful the second time round, as now you're part of a chain.

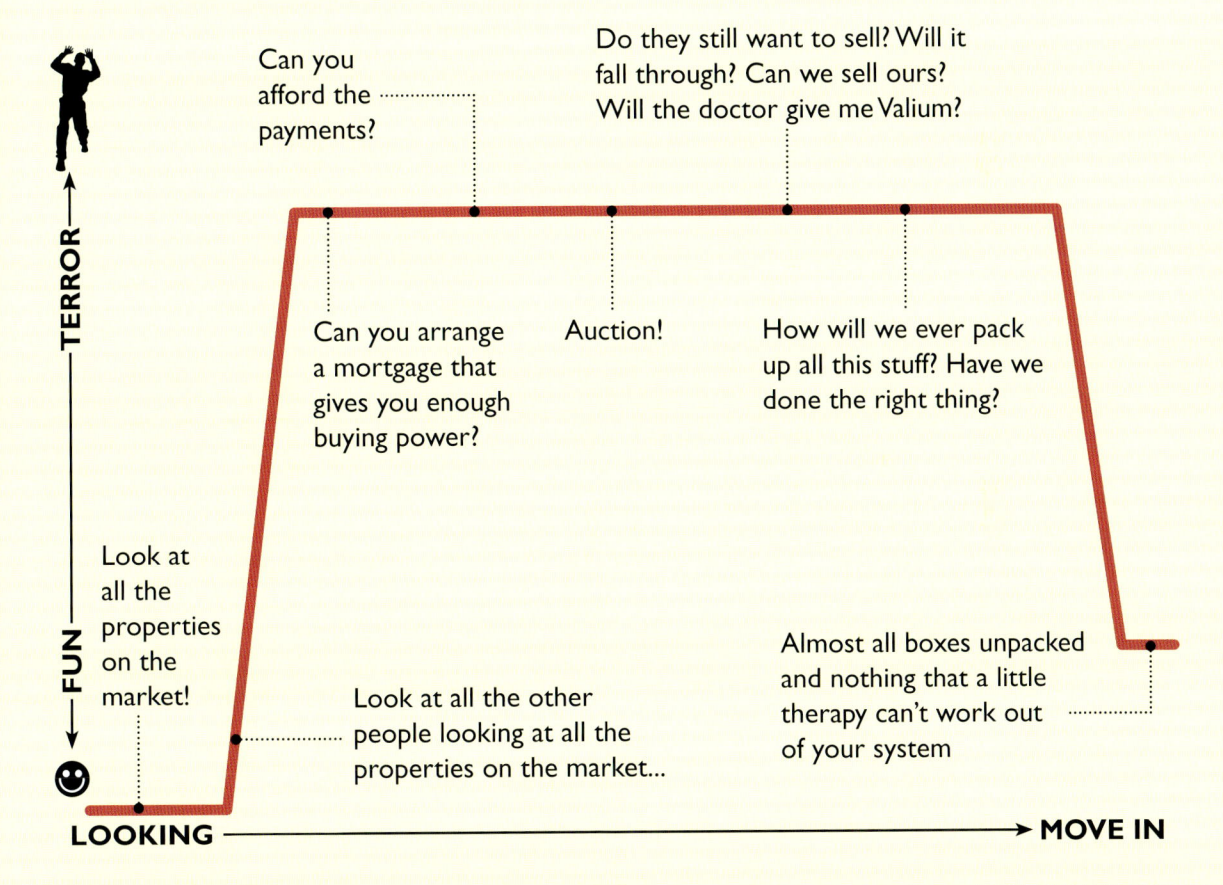

TERROR ← → FUN

- Look at all the properties on the market!
- Can you arrange a mortgage that gives you enough buying power?
- Can you afford the payments?
- Look at all the other people looking at all the properties on the market...
- Auction!
- Do they still want to sell? Will it fall through? Can we sell ours? Will the doctor give me Valium?
- How will we ever pack up all this stuff? Have we done the right thing?
- Almost all boxes unpacked and nothing that a little therapy can't work out of your system

LOOKING ⟶ MOVE IN

> On the positive side of things, if you can deal with the ongoing stress levels that are generated by buying and selling properties, then the divorce inevitably resulting from moving-related arguments will feel like an absolute breeze.

Real Man's Stuff

93 Cars: An Idiot's Guide
94 DIY: Difficulty/Praise Ratio
95 DIY: How Handy Are you?
96 Garden: Tool/Fun Ratio
97 Fashion: What We Wear
98 Fashion: Textbook Errors
99 Grooming Basics

Cars: An Idiot's Guide

There is a strong chance that you're a fan of the automobile, and therefore there is no need for advice in this area. If like the author, however, you love everything about *Top Gear* apart from the cars, then you may identify with these basic motoring tips:

Judge a Book by Its Cover

Torque: 240Nm @ 5000rpm, means as much to many of us as saying hello in Sudanese. The author bought his current car (Honda CRV) because it looked a bit like a 4WD, could fit all the child car seats, was within the price range, and the floor of the boot lifted out to make a picnic table. (In voice of Homer Simpson: 'Wow, a table. I'll take it!')

Petrol Cap on the Left; Indicators on the Right

In general this seems to be the case, although sometimes when driving a hire car you manage to flick on the windscreen wipers on a sunny day when flapping for the indicator at a busy junction. Likewise with hire cars the button to flick the petrol cap open is more elusive than the G-spot. It can take 10 minutes before you realise there isn't one and you just unscrew the cap.

Check Water, Oil & Tyre Pressures

Even the most basic drivers can manage these three. Our dads used to be able to change a gearbox; we sometimes pay someone to clean our car. Even so, if the car breaks down, flick the bonnet and have a look in there anyway. It's the thing to do.

All Car Air Fresheners Smell Bad

Orange smells like Grandma's favourite perfume. When will they invent a car freshener that smells like you've just taken home a Chinese takeaway? Eau de KFC?*

It's Never the Little End that Goes

There are three price ranges for repairs: a) It'll take 5 minutes, I've got one here ($37.50); that rises to b) It's not a huge job (but it's still $475...); and finally c) Lots of nodding quietly and looking at the engine from a variety of angles ($2000). Why is it always the big end that goes? Hasn't that got more to wear out than the little one?

*The author would like a cut of the profits if anyone invents this. Most of his friends believe it's a terrible idea.

DIY: Difficulty/Praise Ratio

A study recently found that women find men who do housework sexy. **WARNING:** This is a scam, do not believe it. This has been developed by women in the belief that they can get you cleaning the bath. Different jobs win different brownie points though; here is the scale:

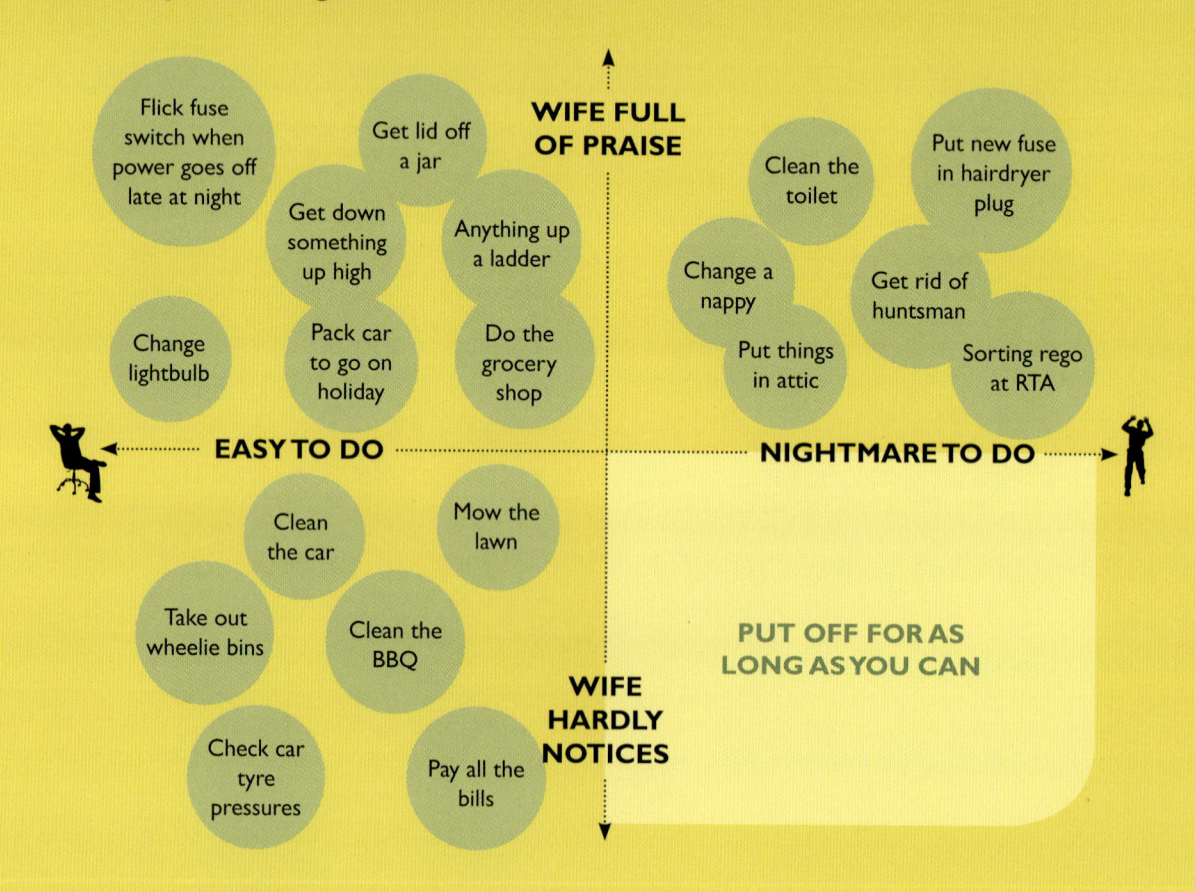

WIFE FULL OF PRAISE

- Flick fuse switch when power goes off late at night
- Get lid off a jar
- Get down something up high
- Anything up a ladder
- Change lightbulb
- Pack car to go on holiday
- Do the grocery shop
- Clean the toilet
- Put new fuse in hairdryer plug
- Change a nappy
- Get rid of huntsman
- Put things in attic
- Sorting rego at RTA

← EASY TO DO   **NIGHTMARE TO DO →**

- Clean the car
- Mow the lawn
- Take out wheelie bins
- Clean the BBQ
- Check car tyre pressures
- Pay all the bills

PUT OFF FOR AS LONG AS YOU CAN

WIFE HARDLY NOTICES

As well as using this chart as potential collateral in getting sex, you can also trade chores against other pleasures, eg do the ironing for two hours while watching the footy on TV on Sunday afternoon.

DIY: How Handy Are You?

Your dad owned overalls. He had a garage with more tools than **Bunnings**, some of which you only see at antiques fairs these days. You have an over-sized fishing tackle box filled with **Allen** keys and brackets from things you made and didn't want to throw out.

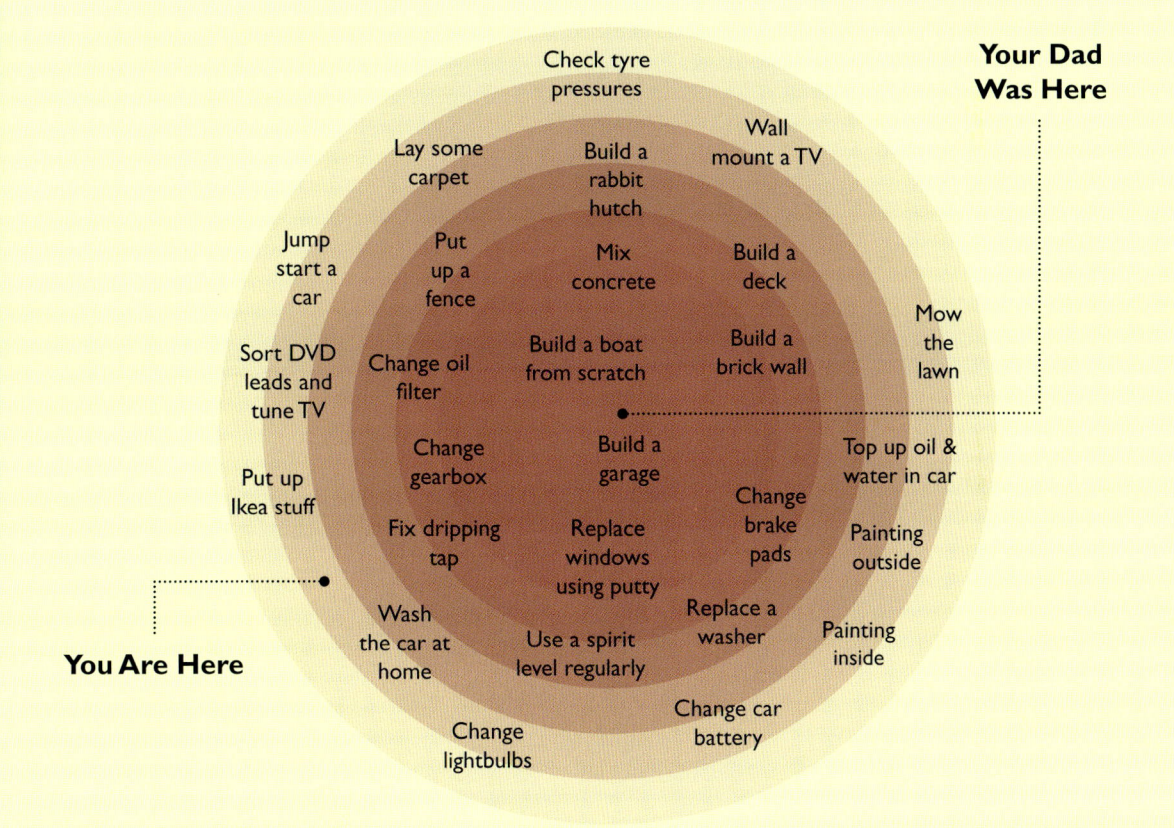

Your Dad Was Here (outer ring):
- Check tyre pressures
- Wall mount a TV
- Mow the lawn
- Top up oil & water in car
- Painting outside
- Painting inside
- Change car battery
- Change lightbulbs
- Use a spirit level regularly
- Wash the car at home
- Put up Ikea stuff
- Sort DVD leads and tune TV
- Jump start a car
- Lay some carpet

Middle ring:
- Build a rabbit hutch
- Build a deck
- Build a brick wall
- Change brake pads
- Replace a washer
- Replace windows using putty
- Fix dripping tap
- Change gearbox
- Change oil filter
- Put up a fence

Inner ring:
- Mix concrete
- Build a boat from scratch
- Build a garage

You Are Here (outside the rings)

The jobs listed above are not necessarily what you're capable of (you can do anything if you put your mind to it), but they're what you actually try yourself, rather than get a bloke in. You could probably carve something ornate for a cathedral if only you had the time.*

*The author would one day like to build a bookshelf-secret-door, like in mystery films. But hasn't got the right tools...

Garden: Tool/Fun Ratio

We may not be that handy with a chisel or a socket set, but we know our way round a backyard. A pair of gardening gloves and a whiff of two-stroke and we feel like a real man. Ready for fun?

TOOL	COST	EASY TO USE	MANLY TO USE	FUN FACTOR (OUT OF 10)	OVERVIEW*
Lawnmower	$$$	👍👍👍	👍👍	7	The manly bit is pulling the starter, from then on it's like pushing a grass-cutting pram. Nice making those lines though.
Leaf Blower	$$$	👍	👍👍👍	9	You feel like a ghostbuster in your own backyard, and any leaf disappears when you shoot. You're a garden magician!
Water Hose	$$$	👍👍👍	👍	10	Gets really good when you put your thumb over the end and speed the jet up. Spray the kids to feel like a real dad.
Hoe	no idea			0	Has anyone used one since the UK Industrial Revolution in the 18th century? Just for getting balls off the roof.
Shears	$$	👍		4	Not as much fun as they look, and trying to cut grass is like trying to cut up fairy floss with nail scissors. Irritating.
Rake	$$			1	Drives you mad as it snags on things. The plastic ones are pathetic. Quicker to use your hands. Garden fail!
Spade	$$	👍👍👍	👍👍	6	Again, flatters to deceive. Starting a hole is fun – that first tread on the blade into turf feels tough. Then it gets boring.

Wheelbarrows, chainsaws and watering cans are also a lot of fun. And obviously axes are excellent. Strimmers are pretty good too (apart from changing the string). In fact a lot of fun can be had with garden tools, if it wasn't for the fact you have to do the garden.

Fashion: What We Wear

In case you didn't get the memo, here's what we're all wearing at the moment. And will be for the next decade at least.

TYPE OF CLOTHING	WHAT YOU'VE GOT IN THE WARDROBE	SMART WEAR	WORK WEAR	CASUAL WEAR	CAN'T BE ARSED
SHOES	Thongs / Nice sandals / Trainers / Smart shoes (trendy) / Smart shoes (boring)	Boring smart shoes to awards dinners or to weddings and christenings	Boring smart shoes (Mon–Thu), trendy smart shoes on Friday	Jeans with trainers to pub, sandals to BBQ, thongs to beach	Thongs or Uggs depending on the weather. With tracky dacks
SHORTS	Board shorts / Cargo shorts / Smart shorts	Smart shorts to a casual christening if you think you can get away with it	Smart shorts to work only on deserted days in summer	Cargo shorts to summer BBQs, boardies to the beach	Boardies with thongs all the time
JEANS	Casual jeans / Smart Jeans	Smart jeans with a jacket if you can pull it off	Smart jeans on a Friday (or all week if you're in the media)	Casual jeans most of time. Trendy shoes with jeans some evenings	Casual jeans with thongs if tracky dacks in the wash
SHIRTS	T-shirts / Polo shirts / Casual slightly trendy shirts / Work shirts / Party shirts	Party shirts or smarter work shirts to formal events. Tucked in	Work shirts tucked in all week, casual shirts untucked on a Friday	Polos or casual shirts with cargo shorts or jeans	T-shirts all the time. In fact the same T-shirt all the time
SMART	Suit / Jacket to go with jeans / Ties (rarely worn) / Bow tie (not sure where it even is)	Suit to wedding, but never with tie. Black tie to Black Tie events (not bow)	Suit on Monday to Thursday, jacket with jeans on a Friday	Jacket with jeans and trainers if feeling confident	Yeah, right
OZ BASICS	Ugg boots / Blunnies / Tracky dacks / Fleece / PJ shorts / Singlet	Not really applicable	Nor here	Still pushing it	All of it
EXTRAS	Belt / Cufflinks / Smart watch / Scruffy watch / Wedding ring (possibly)	All of it worn apart from the scruffy watch	All of it worn apart from the scruffy watch	Scruffy watch and wedding ring	Whatever you can be bothered with
HEAD	Baseball cap / Beanie / Sunnies	Sunnies if needed	Sunnies if needed	Sunnies and cap	Whatever you fancy
SPORTS	Gym gear / Swimmers / Golf gear / Wetsuit / Cycle gear / Walking gear	Would have to be a pretty out-there sort of wedding	Nope	Some of it is applicable depending on what you're up to	Whatever you fancy

Like renaissance men, we're comfortable in a decent suit, but equally comfy in Ugg boots and tracky dacks walking around IGA.

Fashion: Textbook Errors

Some fashion mistakes are obvious: socks with sandals; Harry-high-pants, with the knock-on ankle-cooler effects; white socks. But here are the more subtle fashion traps that men of our age fall into.

Shop in the Right Place

Forget Armani, Gucci, D&G, etc; they're for single men without kids. We're fine in Myer, DJs, Ralph Lauren and Country Road. Kmart and Big W are fine for the Oz Basics mentioned on previous page. Probably too old for Tarocash and Jay Jays; probably got just enough disposable cash to avoid Best & Less.

Avoid Skinny Fit

Even slim fit and tailored fit do us no favours. If you really want the shirt then go up about three normal sizes. This tactic doesn't work with jeans, though – they're like clown's pants round the waist and you still can't get the thigh bits over your calves.

Too Loose is as Bad as Too Tight

We know you're worried about that stomach, but don't look like the kid in the oversized suit when Tom Hanks turns back in *Big*.

XL Doesn't Always Mean XL

Much as we hate trying on clothes (it's like our own personal little Trinny & Susannah humiliation session), it's best to in shops you rarely frequent. The trendier the shop the less likely that XL will be what you expect.

Don't Buy Loud Shirts On Impulse*

An elaborate pink and purple flower pattern, with hidden buttons and a quirky collar. Seemed like a good idea at the time; looks ridiculous stood in front of the mirror an hour before the work Xmas party starts.

Don't Get Crocs

Just don't. What are you, some struggling artist in the back streets of Amsterdam?

Avoid 'Comedy' Clothes

Disney ties, bright-patterned socks, football shirts, World's Greatest Dad T-shirts...

*The author has at least five variations of these – XL, never worn, if anyone's interested.

Grooming Basics

Your daily grooming routine should take 15 minutes at most, including shower,* shave and getting dressed. No haircut should be more than $30. Your hairdresser should either be male and know a lot about footy, or female, under 25 and very good looking. Here are some basic tips:

Hair (Facial)
At your age, if you need to read articles on 'How to have the perfect shave' you're in big f-ing trouble. You might as well read about how to tie your shoelaces. Put on some lubricant (shower gel if there's nothing else), then scrape razor across face until all hair is gone. Ta da! Put on a bit of moisturiser afterwards if you need it or splash cold water if you don't. Don't slap on aftershave. It hurts. Do the Movember thing, by all means, but keep all hair off the rest of the time. Get a nasal trimmer to sort out the nostrils and ears (although there is a perverse pleasure in plucking nasal hair while stopped at traffic lights – a bit like a Wasabi sneeze). And keep the eyebrows in check every so often. The monobrow makes you look slightly deranged. Sideburns can be a dilemma – look at other people for ideas if you're worried about length.

Products
A bit of cologne (the same one you've worn for 15 years); deodorant; hair wax (possibly); moisturiser (at a push); mouthwash, floss and toothpaste; razors. The End.

Hair (Head)
Short at the back, short at the sides, and, frankly, not that long on top either. Slightly roughed up on top to give a devil-may-care feel (as if). If you're losing your hair then cut the rest in sympathy. Avoid too much gel – you're not a 19-year-old working at Crazy John's. If your hair takes more than a minute to style then get a new haircut.

Nails
Keep them short with clippers or scissors after showering. Alternatively, bite them off in the car and flick them out the window, or bite them in front of the TV and flick them behind the sofa. Try not to do the same with toenails. Especially if driving.

Waxing /Spray Tans
You're kidding, right?

*This includes optional masturbation as detailed back on page 66.

Man Time/Leisure

101 Family Activities
102 Holiday Matrix
103 Evenings Out
104 Hobbies Criteria
105 Pyramid of Desire
106 Are You Chef-Like?
107 Music
108 Comfort Films
109 Books We Read
110 How Techy Are We?
111 Why We're Still Highbrow(ish)

Family Activities

There will come a time where kids dominate your life to such an extent that when it comes to choosing to do something that both you and the wife like doing, but that the kids have no interest in, all you can come up with is having a lie-in.

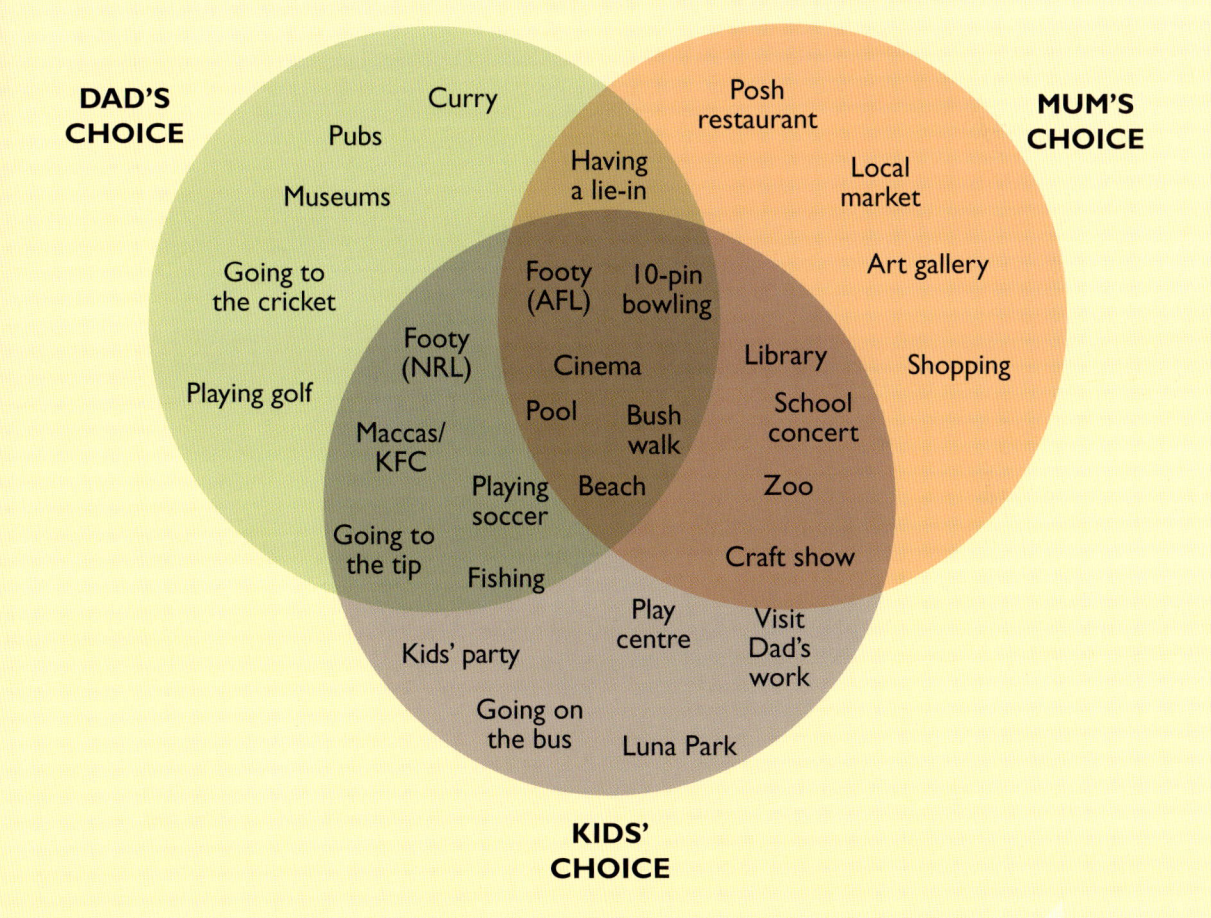

DAD'S CHOICE
- Curry
- Pubs
- Museums
- Going to the cricket
- Playing golf

MUM'S CHOICE
- Posh restaurant
- Local market
- Art gallery
- Shopping

KIDS' CHOICE
- Kids' party
- Going on the bus
- Luna Park

Dad ∩ Mum:
- Having a lie-in

Dad ∩ Kids:
- Footy (NRL)
- Maccas/KFC
- Going to the tip
- Playing soccer
- Fishing

Mum ∩ Kids:
- Library
- School concert
- Zoo
- Craft show
- Visit Dad's work

All three:
- Footy (AFL)
- 10-pin bowling
- Cinema
- Pool
- Bush walk
- Beach
- Play centre

When we die, it is possible that Hell will be a softplay centre run by the devil. An infernal warehouse full of padding in primary colours; the hideous, endless shrieks of children; and tasteless, overpriced coffee.

Holiday Matrix

Tough choices: pitch your Big W 23-man tent at the big holiday park that feels like a refugee camp with a decent pool; or suffer the drunken walk of shame coming home pissed to your babysitting parents.

Type of Holiday	EXXY?	KIDS LOVE IT?	YOU LOVE IT?	OK if it rains?	Low points
Remote Camping	💵	👍	👍	No, it's terrible	Lying on a slowly deflating mattress while holding in a pee for five hours until it's light enough to see the snakes.
Holiday Park Camping	💵💵	👍	👎	Still stuffed	Stilted chat with another bloke while cleaning your teeth in the toilet block, both gamely ignoring the guy you hear taking a dump a metre away.
Holiday Park Cabin	💵💵💵	👍	👍	Just slightly mizzo	Unable to sleep for fear your child will plummet to their death from the bunk bed 15 feet off the ground, with a lip like an infinity pool, rather than railings.
Hotel	💵💵💵	👎	👍	You all go stir crazy	The kids having a massive fight in the middle of the crowded restaurant, just when you thought they might cope. And you're only waiting for starters.
Stay with Parents*		👍	👎	Even more stir crazy	Great to see the folks, but you end up acting like you're 14 again, even if they don't treat you that way. Nightmare when the kids drop the f-bomb.
Resort	💵💵💵💵	👍	👍	Kids club rocks!	Like the holiday park but without the bogans and communal loos. It's expensive, but you get to enjoy your holiday and the kids get to enjoy their holiday.
Cottage	💵💵	👍	👍	It's cosy, not crazy	Probably the best bet all round. Affordable, comfortable, but essentially it's just like being at home somewhere else.

> It's actually interesting to define what constitutes 'camping'. Surely if you turn up with a generator, the dog, a full-sized fridge and a satellite dish, you're hardly 'at one with nature'.

*The author would like to point out to his proud parents that he loves coming home to stay.

Evenings Out

Evenings out with mates take on a whole new complexion when you have kids. After going out three or four nights a week pre-children, you now try to squeeze all four of those nights into one evening. It can get a little messy. And you won't get a lie-in tomorrow.

WITH WIFE... — 7:00PM — WITH MATES...

Venue: Nice little bar
Drink: Beers 1 & 2
Food: No
Chat: The Kids

Venue: Pub
Drink: Beers 1, 2 & 3
Food: Eating's cheating
Chat: How's work? Property prices.

8:00PM

Venue: Booked restaurant
Drink: Wine with meal
Food: Starters
Chat: The Kids

Venue: Pub
Drink: Beers 4, 5 & 6; got a thirst on
Food: Nah
Chat: Sport

9:00PM

Venue: Restaurant
Drink: Wine with meal
Food: Main course
Chat: The Kids

Venue: Pub
Drink: Beers 7 & 8, pretty pissed
Food: Crisps and nuts, in a bid to soak up some booze
Chat: That barmaid is nice

10:00PM

Venue: Restaurant
Drink: Coffee
Food: Just a small dessert
Chat: Other people's marriages

Venue: Pub
Drink: Shots 1 & 2
Food: Nope
Chat: Remember the good old days?

11:00PM

Venue: Taxi home to sitter
Drink: Done
Food: Full
Chat: We ought to do that more often

Venue: Pub
Drink: Shots 3 & 4
Food: No, let's go grab a curry
Chat: But what am I really doing with my life?

LATER...

Venue: Bed
Drink: No
Food: No
Chat: Quickie?

Venue: Indian restaurant
Drink: Order beer, have one sip, then drink water
Food: Curry
Chat: You're the best mate I've ever had...

More restrained when out with your partner, as you've got to talk to the babysitter later (possibly the daughter of other friends). Plus too many drinks and that simmering child-related tension will kick off.

Hobbies Criteria

We've concentrated on sporting hobbies, even though for many men cooking, cars or playing the guitar is their thing. For this table we're interested in the Great Outdoors rather than the Great Indoors.

HOBBY	EXXY?	ALCOHOL INVOLVED?	FITNESS REQUIRED?	FLATTERING CLOTHES?	VERDICT
GOLF	$$$	Of course, 19th hole. Maybe 20th	Gets tiring on a par 5th 14th hole. But, no.	Shorts, polo shirts; it's like a BBQ. Fine	If you take it up now you'll be okay by the time you retire. Gentle fun, easy to chat
CYCLING	$$$	Seem to drink coffee, not beer	Yeah, they pedal for miles	Don't buy the lycra until you're fitter	It's the new golf. Take up half the road on a bike, then sit outside a coffee shop in lycra
OVER-35s SOCCER	$	By the side of the pitch. (Afterwards)	Yes. And check your life cover	Why are those shirts so tight?	Great fun and you can sub on and off frequently if you need it. And you do need it
HIKING	$$	An ale at the local tavern after a trek	Depends if it's Kosciuszko or Everest	Pretty cool, and with zips everywhere	Great gear, especially if you're camping. Feel a little bit like Bear Grylls
SURFING	$$$	More of a morning thing	Yep, those guys look ripped	Wetsuits can do you some favours	If you can't do it by now then it's hard. Plus there's the whole shark thing...
MARTIAL ARTS	$	No way! Your body is zen-like	Tough as nails	Baggy white PJs and a belt. Okay	Every time you watch *Karate Kid* you're tempted. Great for potential road-rage incidents
RUNNING	$	One beer to collapse after races	If you do half-marathons, then yes	Depends how fit and how much lycra	The weight just falls off, but you can't breathe for the first 20 or so runs

Eventually it'll be lawn bowls and writing letters of complaint to the local council that takes up your leisure time, but for now make the most of that just-about-functioning body. If you really can't hack sport then maybe try trend-setting by bringing back smoking a pipe.

Pyramid of Desire

We love buying toys. The garage is full of sports gear we've collected over the years. And there's always the next thing waiting on eBay for our attention. We'd like the following:

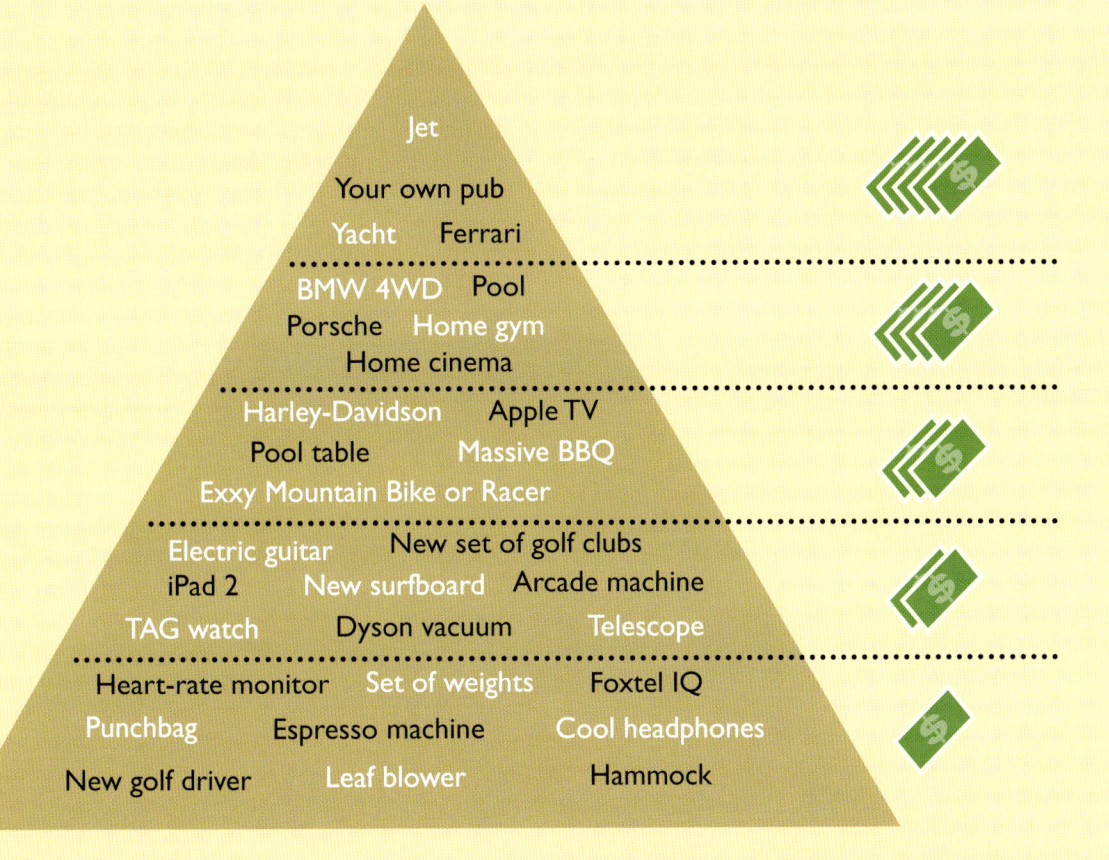

- Jet
- Your own pub
- Yacht   Ferrari
- BMW 4WD   Pool
- Porsche   Home gym
- Home cinema
- Harley-Davidson   Apple TV
- Pool table   Massive BBQ
- Exxy Mountain Bike or Racer
- Electric guitar   New set of golf clubs
- iPad 2   New surfboard   Arcade machine
- TAG watch   Dyson vacuum   Telescope
- Heart-rate monitor   Set of weights   Foxtel IQ
- Punchbag   Espresso machine   Cool headphones
- New golf driver   Leaf blower   Hammock

> We've made the assumption that everyone has an iPhone and therefore there is no need to crave a camera, **GPS** or video camera. And the second assumption is that only females like the Kindle. Like much of the book, there's no real science behind that, it's just a vibe.

Are You Chef-Like?

The idea portrayed in adverts that men can't cook is ludicrous. Does anyone watch the presenters on *Masterchef*? It's Maggie Beer and a bunch of blokes. We do okay at home too. Take the test below to see how you compare to your peers in the kitchen:

Start

- How many Jamie Oliver books do you own? *(1 point for each book)*
- Do you ever get weepy during *Masterchef*? *(5 points)*
- Have you made any of the following from scratch (not using a jar of sauce): Indian curry, Thai curry, Bolognese, stir fry? *(1 point for each)*
- Have you made any of the following from scratch: risotto, full roast, shepherd's pie, apple crumble? *(2 points for each)*
- Have you ever made your own chicken stock from scratch? *(5 points)*
- Have you made your own pasta in the past? *(5 points)*
- Have you made any of the following from scratch: sushi, chocolate mousse cake, twice-cooked pork belly, confit of salmon? *(3 points for each)*
- Have you considered buying a small blow-torch for the kitchen? *(10 points)*
- Can you make decent tempura batter that actually stays on? *(5 points)*
- Do you cook steak: rare *(2 points)*, medium rare *(3 points)*, well done *(1 point)*?
- Do you clean up the kitchen as you go? *(5 points)*
- Do you always use chopsticks when eating Chinese food at home? *(3 points)*
- You get home late from work and rather than ordering take away, you throw something great together from leftovers in the fridge? *(10 points)*

Finish

- **75+ POINTS**: Wow, shave your head and get some distinctive eyewear, aren't you Heston Blumenthal?
- **40-74 POINTS**: Wow, shave your head and get a tough attitude, aren't you Matt Moran?
- **0-39 POINTS**: Wow, shave your head and get a Duff beer, aren't you Homer Simpson?

Music

One of the many ways in which we have become our own fathers is that we shake our heads sadly at the music videos our children watch on MTV and wonder why we can't understand the lyrics. Instead we listen to:

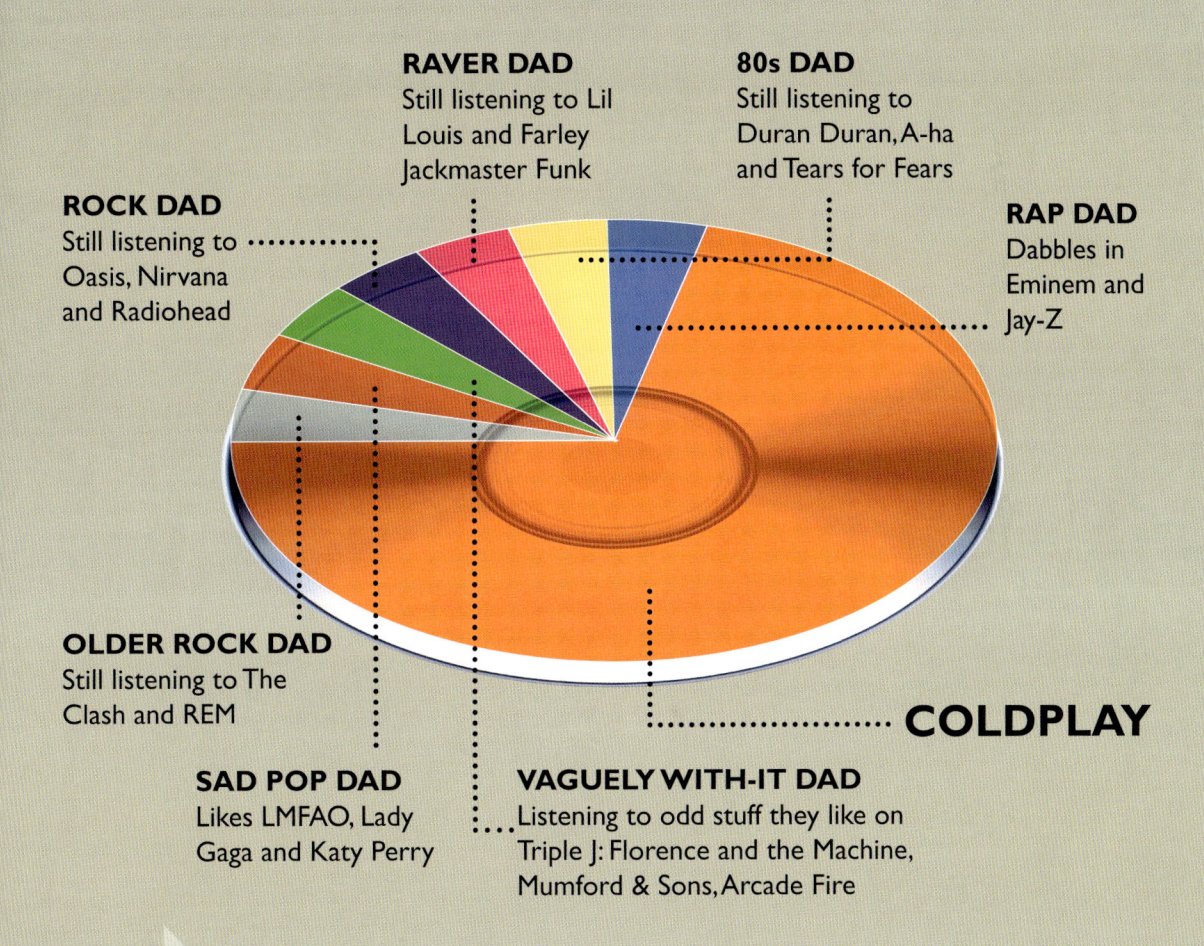

RAVER DAD
Still listening to Lil Louis and Farley Jackmaster Funk

80s DAD
Still listening to Duran Duran, A-ha and Tears for Fears

ROCK DAD
Still listening to Oasis, Nirvana and Radiohead

RAP DAD
Dabbles in Eminem and Jay-Z

OLDER ROCK DAD
Still listening to The Clash and REM

COLDPLAY

SAD POP DAD
Likes LMFAO, Lady Gaga and Katy Perry

VAGUELY WITH-IT DAD
Listening to odd stuff they like on Triple J: Florence and the Machine, Mumford & Sons, Arcade Fire

Even if we're still listening to decent music, we lose the ability to dance at around the age of 29. From then on we shuffle and convulse ironically at weddings every year or two, but only if very drunk.

Comfort Films

Why watch a new movie when you can watch one you've seen 37 times already? You can mouth the words to the best bits ('You can't **HANDLE** the truth'), and you can prepare properly for the weepy bits. Here is a list of some of our favourite comfort films:

A Few Good Men Pulp Fiction Gladiator
Die Hard The Castle (cry like a baby) Star Wars Casino Back to the Future
The Bourne Films Monty Python and The Holy Grail
Layer Cake Planes, Trains & Automobiles Any James Bond Movie
Spinal Tap Trainspotting The Hunt For Red October
Field of Dreams Goodfellas The Italian Job City Slickers Big
Monty Python and the Life of Brian
Rocky The Departed LA Confidential Apocalypse Now
Crocodile Dundee
When Harry Met Sally Rushmore The Great Escape
All The President's Men Jaws Reservoir Dogs High Fidelity
The Magnificent Seven It's A Wonderful Life (cry like a baby)
12 Angry Men Withnail and I Groundhog Day Spartacus
Notting Hill (No, really) Snatch
Godfather 2 Muppet Christmas Carol (!!) Midnight Run Godfather
The Dish Zulu The Shawshank Redemption Sideways
Top Gun
Heat Close Encounters of the Third Kind Jerry Maguire Speed
Love Actually (Again, not joking) Grosse Point Blank
The Good, The Bad and The Ugly Lock, Stock and Two Smoking Barrels

> The really weird thing is that we'll stay up to almost midnight on a week night just to see the end of a film that we've already seen 30 times – even if we own it on **DVD** anyway.

Books We Read

After reading Kafka and Kerouac in our youth, we settle into a life of crime (so to speak) in our thirties. And who needs Albert Camus or Truman Capote when there's Wayne Carey and Shane Crawford?

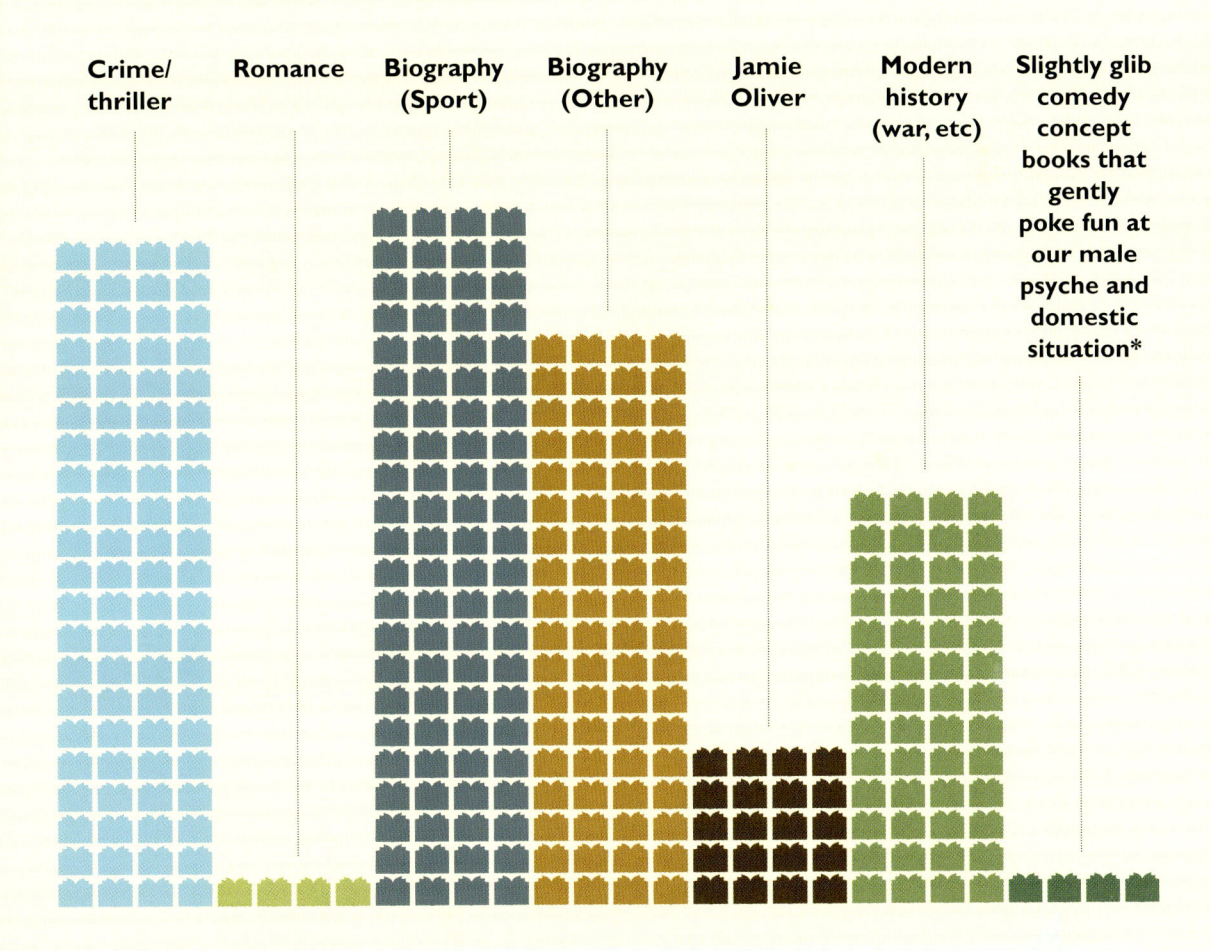

| Crime/thriller | Romance | Biography (Sport) | Biography (Other) | Jamie Oliver | Modern history (war, etc) | Slightly glib comedy concept books that gently poke fun at our male psyche and domestic situation* |

Obviously books aren't our only reading material. We also religiously read the back pages of the newspapers, and some of the stuff at the front. And we love a look at the Bunnings and IKEA catalogues.

*The author would like to point out that he has a family to support, so if we could push this column up a little...

How Techy Are We?

We love technology and gravitate toward gadgets, but are wary of the speed at which it evolves. It irritates us that there is a pile of videos in the cupboard that we will never play again, and yet cannot throw out. And we're still not sure whether Blu-ray will stick around.

Progress through the following questions to see whether you're as savvy with computers as your 10-year-old son.

- Do you download tracks on iTunes?
- Have you sold stuff on eBay?
- Have you built your own website?
- Do you post on Facebook more than once a week?
- Have you bought stuff on eBay?
- Do you look at YouTube regularly?
- Have you got an iPad?
- Have you played a Wii?
- Have you got a Facebook account?
- Do you post regularly on Twitter?
- Do you record and series-link TV shows on Foxtel?
- Did you camp outside the Apple store to get an iPad 2, video the whole thing on your iPhone, dub a relevant track over the top and then post it alongside a blog on your website; then share a link to that on your Twitter account; then share a link to all of that on your Facebook account with a check-in at the Apple Store; while at the same time monitoring whether anyone had bought your original iPad on eBay?
- Have you got an iPod?
- Can you tune a new TV in AND sort which lead goes where?
- Did you upgrade from iPad to iPad2?

Despite exposure to all these cutting-edge platforms, we still bang shut the front of the photocopier to try and fix it; and we always ask someone to help us use the fax ('So, do I push zero first? Do they face up or down?'). Why isn't there an iFax for God's sake?

Why We're Still Highbrow(ish)

At uni we watched Peter Greenaway films (especially if there was the chance of a shag afterwards). Since having children, we've started getting weepy at *The Biggest Loser* and have actually enjoyed at least four Adam Sandler films. There are still a few things we cling to, though, that we hope make us culturally relevant.

- We loved *The West Wing*, enjoy *Mad Men* and like *The Wire*, although the street talk is a bit tricky to understand.

- We saw *The King's Speech* at the cinema. We felt really culturally good about ourselves that night.

- We've seen *The Seven Samurai* on DVD. Bit long, and preferred *The Magnificent Seven*, to be honest.

- We quote things from films like *Trainspotting* and *Pulp Fiction* when we get the chance. Admittedly it's trite stuff like: 'Bacon tastes gooood. Pork chops taste gooood.'

- We buy a broadsheet sometimes and read the entertainment section. We read the sport first, of course, and don't even bother with the main news part. But all the same.

- We listen to AM and PM on ABC local radio when driving to work and home again. We know about debt crisis, okay?

- We watch films that have subtitles. (Especially if we anticipate sex scenes.)

- We read *Atonement* by Ian McEwan and not only understood it, but actually enjoyed it.

- We wear reading glasses. That means we're smart, right?

- We know that Gotye came top of Triple J's Hottest 100. It's catchy. Sounds a bit like The Police.

- We have framed art in the house. Some of it modern art. Accessible stuff like Paul Klee or Mark Rothko, probably purchased from a poster place and framed. But it's art all the same.

Okay, so we're middlebrow at best, but at least we don't watch *Home and Away* anymore. Unless it happens to be on...

"Sometimes things have to get worse before they get better, but when you really feel at your lowest, it can be the time when the window of opportunity opens wide enough for you to seize the moment."

Conclusions & Next Steps

115 Summary
116 We're Not This
117 So What Are We Really?
118 Next Steps

Summary

Like many of my real business reports this has been largely devoid of decent research, incisive facts and radical conclusions. But it's suitably long, reasonably well written and on nice paper. Job done. Here are a few random things we've learned from the book, though.

- That when the pressure gets too much, shit comes out sideways and you'll even welcome the idea of a temporary coma.

- That none of our mates are called Cody and none of our school friends grew up to become stunt men.

- That if you haven't a) learned to surf, or b) started a pension by now, then it may be a little late for either.

- That, frankly, Dad needs to take a chill pill, as he's often chucking a spaz.

- That whether you like it or not, your function in life is to facilitate family life.

- That love, sex and friendship are all possible at once, but jeez it's a big ask over a long period of time.

- That masturbation never, ever lets you down.

- That all car air fresheners smell really, really bad.

- That diets do work, but only if you actually follow them.

- That we all like pork belly and duck. And we will happily pick something off the floor to eat it if we feel it was only dropped in the last 24 hours.

- That we will all go nuts eventually.*

- That kids are very expensive. (Yeah, like you learned that from the book!)

- That *Hansel and Gretel* is not a good bedtime story. And that cheap AND relaxed birthday parties do not exist.

- That two days' sick leave is more believable than one.

- That if you need a dump and one cubicle is already occupied in an intimate 2-cubicle toilet, then for the Love of God, walk away.

I mean, I could go on, but the page has been filled. Yet again, job done.

*In my case it happened around page 101 of this book.

We're Not This

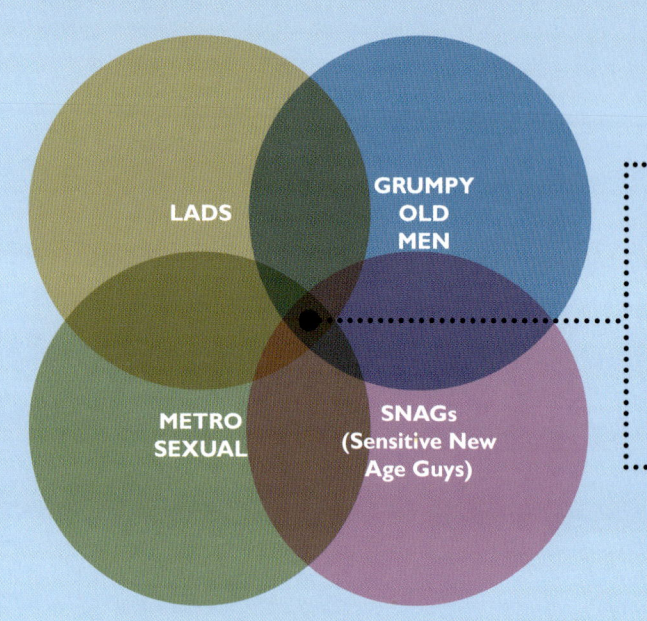

LADS

GRUMPY OLD MEN

METRO SEXUAL

SNAGs (Sensitive New Age Guys)

Of the four most recent attempts at pigeonholing men, there are parts we can identify with in all of the labels. We probably sit in the middle of all of these, and yet that dot signifies a group of people that is far larger than the scale would ever suggest.

FAMILY MAN

The media describes any married man with children as a Family Man, whether he's hands-on with the kids or not.

?

SALARYMAN

In Japan, this stereotype is a white-collar worker whose life is tied to his desk, who binges on drink and karaoke at night.

Again, while there are elements of both of these in our make-up, neither of them accurately tells the story of our lives.

So What Are We Really?

I'm loath to come up with a new acronym or term for men like us. Mainly because after hours of searching for one, I couldn't come up with anything that captured the essence completely. I think that actually tells a story more about us and our differences than my lack of creativity.* Here are some traits that perhaps we all share.

Just because we might love beer, footy, women and spicy food, it doesn't mean that we're 'lads'. Sport is a beautiful thing. So are women. And beer and curry can both scrub up well on their day. We like what we like. Is that really a problem?

We can be 'salarymen' to a certain degree, but we fight against it. The toll that providing for a family in this increasingly material world takes is a really hard one. It's not what we want, but it can become increasingly difficult to control.

Just because we like cooking or do the weekly grocery shop, or read the IKEA catalogue and prefer the house to be tidy, it doesn't mean that we're 'SNAGs'. I like clothes shopping more than my wife does. It is what it is.

We're not grumpy old men, but we've been around a while, and increasingly we don't suffer fools gladly. Of course we get annoyed in traffic or talking to call centres – that's because it's really f-ing annoying.

We love our kids more than anything in the world (even more than sport and beer). We're happy to be hands-on fathers, but sometimes they drive us absolutely nuts and work actually seems appealing. But to leave home, and to not wake up with them on a daily basis, you have to have a bloody good reason. And if we do take that route, it doesn't mean we're no longer Family Men. Kids are our life, for life.

We take an interest in our appearance, be that clothes, fitness or a bit of wax in the hair. But it's really not the thing that drives us.

We're ordinary, good blokes. The same, but different. And the country is full of us.

*I would say that though, wouldn't I?

Next Steps

The next step is whatever you want it to be. No, really, it is. Whatever you think the barriers are to a better life (money, weight, family, career), **it's still in your hands**. It seems incongruous to go all self-help guru on you at this point and ply you with platitudes, with only 500 words to go; but you only get one crack at this life. **If you're not happy then you need to make changes before it's too late**. Sometimes things have to get worse before they get better; but when you really feel at your lowest, it can be the time when the window of opportunity opens wide enough for you to **seize the moment**. If for no other reason than you're scared of what the future looks like for you.

I've taken a slightly glib, glass-half-full approach to almost all of the book, simply because **pathos and self-deprecation make for a better comedic vehicle**. You can't make a funny observational book without empathy, irony, self-mocking and a show of vulnerability. Winners and well-rounded, sincerely happy people are impressive and inspiring, but frankly, they're not funny. **Homer Simpson and George Costanza are a lot funnier than the Dalai Lama or Barack Obama**. This book really comes from a very light take on the place I was in three or four years ago. The change for me was to give up drinking. I'd come to rely on it and it was making me and all of the people around me miserable. **Life had become very narrow for me**; I was depressed, I lacked enthusiasm for almost everything and I really couldn't see a way forward that made sense. So I gave up the one thing that seemed to make me happy – alcohol – and **my life has steadily improved**. I'm nowhere near living the Perfect Schedule back on page 44, but I've got myself fitter and lost some weight over the last few years; my health has improved – mentally and physically. **I love doing things with the kids now and I'm finally the father I wanted to be**. The father I knew I was capable of being, but somehow couldn't achieve. I've changed jobs and enjoy what I do. **I actually like working hard and not acting like an arsehole now**. We've moved house. We go out for family meals, and go to the pool and go to the beach and have fun. **Nothing flash, just simple pleasures**. I wake up in the morning and want to live life, rather than avoid it. And in about 20 minutes' time I'll have finished writing a book, like I always wanted to. If I can do it, so can you. **If I can drag my sorry arse out of the bottle shop and onto the beach for a walk at 6 am, then anyone can**. I'm not special, I was just lucky enough to get a glimpse of who I really was – and it wasn't pretty. I finally learned that it didn't matter what greatness I thought I was capable of if I wasn't doing any of it. **People only perceived me through my behaviour, not the stuff going on in my head**. Now I try to live by the creed that I'm the product of my actions, not my intentions. There are plenty of men out there struggling with their life, when there may not be a need to. When I've discussed this book with others they've visibly slumped and said 'Christ, I'm like that'. A lot of your mates will feel the same. **Don't be afraid to talk to them about it – you'll be surprised at the results**. Don't leave it until the 10th beer of the night to finally say what's bothering you – get it out there early instead of talking about the footy. Women look after each other and share each other's problems; we hold onto them tightly, believing we're the only ones who feel that way. That we're the only ones who can solve our own problems and to ask for help is weak. **In the end it can take us to places we don't want to go**. You can do it, you really can. **Don't be your harshest critic – be your own best friend**. Share a few problems with a mate and start the healing process if it's needed.

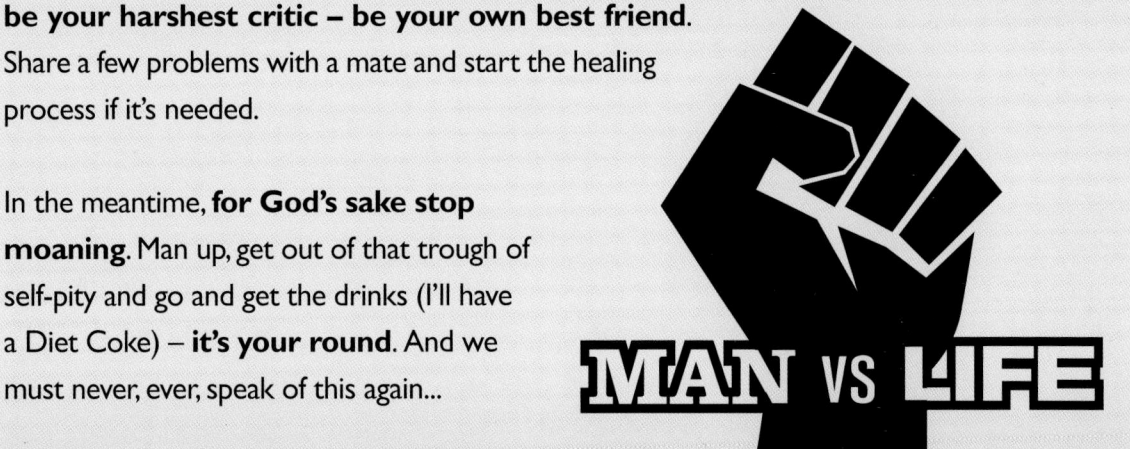

In the meantime, **for God's sake stop moaning**. Man up, get out of that trough of self-pity and go and get the drinks (I'll have a Diet Coke) – **it's your round**. And we must never, ever, speak of this again...

Published in 2012 by Murdoch Books Pty Limited

Murdoch Books Australia
Pier 8/9
23 Hickson Road
Millers Point NSW 2000
Phone: +61 (0) 2 8220 2000
Fax: +61 (0) 2 8220 2558
www.murdochbooks.com.au
info@murdochbooks.com.au

Murdoch Books UK Limited
Erico House, 6th Floor
93–99 Upper Richmond Road
Putney, London SW15 2TG
Phone: +44 (0) 20 8785 5995
Fax: +44 (0) 20 8785 5985
www.murdochbooks.co.uk
info@murdochbooks.co.uk

For Corporate Orders & Custom Publishing contact Noel Hammond, National Business Development Manager, Murdoch Books Australia

Publisher: Tracy Lines
Designer: Russell Whittle
Project manager: Sophia Oravecz
Production: Joan Beal

Text © Rob Pegley
The moral right of the author has been asserted.
Design © Murdoch Books Pty Limited 2012

Every reasonable effort has been made to trace the owners of copyright materials in this book, but in some instances this has proven impossible. The author and publisher will be glad to receive information leading to more complete acknowledgements in subsequent printings of the book and in the meantime extend their apologies for any omissions.

All rights reserved. No part of this publication may be reproduced, stored in a retrieval system or transmitted in any form or by any means, electronic, mechanical, photocopying, recording or otherwise, without the prior written permission of the publisher.

A cataloguing-in-publication entry is available from the catalogue of the National Library of Australia at www.nla.gov.au.

A catalogue record for this book is available from the British Library.

Printed by 1010 Printing International Limited, China